£2

To, Jack /
Happy

Love June
x

28/8/91

Cricket Mercenaries

Cricket Mercenaries

Overseas Players in English Cricket

David Lemmon

PAVILION

MICHAEL JOSEPH

Published in Great Britain in 1987 by
Pavilion Books Limited
196 Shaftesbury Avenue, London WC2H 8JL
in association with Michael Joseph Limited
27 Wrights Lane, Kensington, London W8 5TZ

British Library Cataloguing in Publication Data
Lemmon, David
    Cricket mercenaries.
    1. Cricket – England
    I. Title
    796.35'863'0942   GV928.G7

ISBN 1-85145-134-X

Printed by Anchor Brendon, Tiptree, England

The publishers would like to thank Heinemann Quixote
for permission to reproduce the oil painting by Ivan Rose,
based on a photograph by Adrian Murrell. It previously
appeared in *The Lord's Taverners' 50 Greatest*.

Contents

Illustrations

Preface

When England suffered crushing defeats at the hands of the West Indies, both in England and in the Caribbean, we found it necessary to search for reasons for our failure. The obvious reasons, like the inability of our batsmen to cope with sustained hostile fast bowling of high quality, seemed insufficient, and the scapegoats most commonly chosen were one-day cricket and the presence of overseas cricketers in county cricket who, it was alleged, were hindering the development of home grown players.

Many believe that the problem of overseas players in county cricket is one that has been with us only since 1968 when the immediate registration of cricketers not qualified to represent England was first allowed, but this is far from true. In 1878, W.G. Grace captured Midwinter, born in Gloucestershire but playing for the Australians, from under the noses of the Australian management and sparked a debate which has raged, with varying degrees of passion, ever since. Spofforth and Ferris, great Australian cricketers, represented English counties in the nineteenth century, and at the beginning of this century, the arrival of 'Alberto' Trott and Tarrant and later of the Queensland all-rounder Marshal caused the most heated argument, which was quelled only by the First World War.

In the years between the wars, several cricketers, mostly from Australia, came to England to seek to earn a living at the game, and in the years after the Second World War, Australia lost almost a complete Test side to English county cricket.

The difference between the overseas players who came to England before 1968 and those who have come since is that the first group were men who came searching for a livelihood, the second have been sought by counties who themselves were searching for glamour and success. Not all importations have been wise or successful, and I have attempted to trace not only the history of overseas players in English cricket, but the dilemmas which have faced clubs and individuals because of their presence.

That some have brought success to counties is undeniable, and this was the reason for their importation at a time when the winning of trophies has become an increasingly important part of the game; that others have caused problems and ended the careers of some young English players is also undeniable. In the end, it is the public who has decided, and will continue to decide, whether it is willing to pay to see untried and untested players of doubtful potential or whether it would rather pay to see Richard Hadlee, Mike Procter, Viv Richards or Ken McEwan.

I have tried to point out that, whatever the decision, a price is paid.

Leigh-on-Sea, 1987   David Lemmon

PART 1
The Pioneers

On 19 April 1907, *The Tribune* reported the Annual General Meeting of Essex County Cricket Club. The affairs of the Club were treated in a complimentary, if perfunctory, manner, but the main part of the report was given to a speech made by the Essex Chairman, Mr Charles Ernest Green, who, two years earlier, had been President of MCC.

'Speaking with his forty years' experience of county cricket, Mr Green made a long address on the Colonial importation question. He regretted that the meeting at Lord's had not thought fit to adopt the Essex suggestion for a five years' minimum. But the question was by no means settled.

Mr Green felt that the Australian Colonies, as well as the English counties, were affected by the importation business. It was reducing county cricket from its highest level of sport for clubs to be seeking abroad for players, and he thought that Surrey, with all it's splendid traditions, should at least have been above descending to importation. It was not cricket.'

C.E. Green's angry outburst was occasioned by Surrey's plans to sign the Australian batsman Alan Marshal. It was the culmination of a debate on the ethics of importing overseas cricketers which had raged heatedly for several years. Although the number of importations was small, the argument roused the fiercest passions, for many saw the increasing number of overseas players in county cricket as threatening to the very fabric of the game. Eighty years later, the question has by no means been settled.

The Essex proposition at the meeting of the Advisory Committee of the Counties at Lord's, on 19 December 1906, had been 'That the period for qualification of Colonial cricketers should be for not less than five years.' But this proposition was withdrawn in favour of the one submitted by Kent which read 'The time for qualification be extended for the man who comes to this country for the purpose of making a livelihood out of cricket.'

This proposal, which would have extended the period of residential qualification for overseas cricketers from the existing two years, was defeated by eight votes to seven. Lord Hawke, for Yorkshire, supported the motion. Among those who voted against it were C.B. Fry on behalf of Sussex, J. Horner for Lancashire, J. Shuter for Surrey, and Dr Bencraft for Hampshire. The Middlesex representative, Gregor MacGregor, abstained. All had good reason for voting as they did.

The whole question of registration and qualification saw the counties deeply divided, and although rules were drawn up by the Committee of MCC in February 1907, much was left in abeyance.

The first rules on qualification were drawn up at a meeting in London in December 1872, and were designed to prevent a player from appearing for more than one county in any single season. These rules, which were finally accepted in June 1873, allowed a player to choose at the beginning of a season whether he would play for the county of his birth or the county of his residence. One stipulation was that should he opt to play for the county of his residence, he could not play against the county of his birth. The residential qualification was placed at a duration of three years for professionals and two years for amateurs, but a year later it was made a uniform two years for both classes of cricketer.

A.E. Knight, one of the most articulate of professional cricketers, saw the regulations of 1873 as giving 'a stability and firmness to the whole county cricket of the country'. It was under these regulations that the first overseas player, William Evans Midwinter, came into county cricket. Midwinter was born in Gloucestershire in 1851, but his family emigrated to Australia when he was nine. His father went south in search of gold.

Midwinter senior worked first as a goldminer and then as a butcher. William, between his butcher's rounds, acquired a passion for all games, especially cricket. He was outstanding at most sports, being an excellent quarter-miler, a fine rifle shot and a notable billiards player. As a cricketer, he was a hard-hitting right-handed batsman, a medium-pace right-arm spin bowler and a brilliant outfielder with a strong arm.

At the age of thirteen, he won a place in the Bendigo United senior team. By the age of twenty, he was in the Victoria side and had won fame by bowling both W.G. and G.F. Grace in 1874.

In March 1877, he played for Australia against England in what has become recognised as the first Test Match. He played an important part in the Australian victory, taking five for 78 in the first innings. It is interesting to note that six of that first Australian side were not born in Australia.

At the end of the Australian season, Midwinter came to England and played with W.G. Grace. His first-class debut in England was at Lord's in mid-July when he played, as a professional, for the combined Gloucestershire and Yorkshire side against England. A week later, he played for the South against the North at Hull.

The following day he was at The Oval playing for Gloucestershire in their victory over England. Midwinter took seven for 35 and four for 46, and from that point he was a regular member of the Gloucestershire side for the rest of the season. With seven victories in eight matches, Gloucestershire were declared the champion county.

There was no argument as to Midwinter's right to play for Gloucestershire, for he was representing the county of his birth. The fact that he had played for Australia a few months earlier was of little account. Test matches had not yet taken on the importance that they were to assume later. Indeed, the encounters of 1877 were not sanctified with the name of 'Test match' until several years after they had taken place. The first Australian side to tour England, in 1878, played no international matches.

That Australian side arrived with eleven players and with the intention that Midwinter should bring that number up to twelve. He had begun his season when they arrived, having played for An England XI against Cambridge University, for England against MCC, and for Eleven of England against the Players of the North.

He joined the Australians for their opening first-class match, against Nottinghamshire, and he played in the sensational victory in under five and a half hours over MCC at Lord's. He then played against Yorkshire, Surrey and the Gentlemen of England, and he was practising at Lord's before the game against Middlesex, when W.G. Grace arrived. The 'Champion' insisted that Midwinter should be playing for his native Gloucestershire against Surrey and bundled him into his carriage and drove across London to The Oval.

The Australian manager, Conway, organised a posse to recapture the defector, and Grace and Midwinter were confronted outside The Oval. A heated argument took place in front of an interested crowd, and Grace called the Australians 'a damn lot of sneaks' for trying to bribe Midwinter to break his agreement to play for Gloucestershire. The argument continued in correspondence.

Gloucestershire avowed that Midwinter was 'a Gloucestershire man who had promised Mr Grace to play in all county matches', and that Grace's 'stormy language' was justified because the Australians had attempted to induce Midwinter to break his commitment by offering him more money than the County could afford. Eventually, Grace apologised, but Midwinter played for Gloucestershire for the remainder of the season.

The argument over Midwinter and the coming of the Australians rekindled Grace's fire for the first-class game. He had been suggesting that he might retire because of his medical work and his family commitments, but he was to straddle the game like a Colossus for another quarter of a century.

Midwinter played for Gloucestershire for the next two seasons. After the 1908 season he went to Australia and represented Victoria, so becoming the first commuter cricketer, playing for an English county and in an overseas competition in the same year.

He had now joined the MCC staff of bowlers, and in 1881 he played for both MCC and Gloucestershire. In 1881-82, he was in Alfred Shaw's side that played a Test series in Australia. In the four matches, Midwinter scored 95 runs and took ten wickets.

He played his sixth consecutive season for Gloucestershire in 1882, but he returned to Australia at the end of the season saying that he objected to being called an Anglo-Australian. He asserted that he was Australian to the core. The *Sydney Mail* was sceptical of his patriotism and asked, 'Are we to submit to another season of vagueness from this very slippery cricketer? One day he is an Australian and the next day an English player.'

In fact, Midwinter had played his last game for Gloucestershire, and for MCC. He was welcomed back as an Australian, scored 92 not out for Victoria against Ivo Bligh's side, and played in the fourth Test match of the series – this time for Australia.

He came to England with Murdoch's side in 1884, and he played his last two Tests for Australia against Shrewsbury's side in 1886-87. Three years later he was dead.

The end was tragic. A devoted family man, he saw his three-month-old daughter die of pneumonia in 1888 and his wife die following a stroke a year later. Three months after the death of his wife, he lost his son and, unable to bear these grievous losses, he broke down and was committed to a mental institution in Melbourne where he died in 1890 at the age of 39.

Under the existing regulations, there was never any question about Midwinter's eligibility to play for Gloucestershire, and it was in Australia that his loyalties were viewed with some misapprehension, but, as we have noted, most of Australia's players in the early Tests had strong family ties in England. Midwinter remains the only cricketer to have played for Australia against England, and for England against Australia.

He was not the last Australian Test player to be seduced by the charms of Gloucestershire and the personality of W.G. Grace. A decade after he had played his last game for the county, Gloucestershire had acquired the services of John James Ferris.

Ferris's left-arm bowling had struck fear into the hearts of English batsmen in 1888 and 1890. In conjunction with C.T.B. Turner, he formed one of the most lethal of Test opening attacks. On the tour of 1888, Ferris took 199 wickets, and two years later he took 186. It was on this second tour to England that he agreed to qualify for Gloucestershire so that his last Test for Australia was at The Oval in 1890.

He went back to Sydney to settle his business affairs before beginning his new career and was inundated by requests and gifts from people who beseeched him to remain in Australia. In retrospect, he may have wished that he had listened to their pleas.

15

While qualifying for Gloucestershire he went to South Africa with W.W. Read's team and had a highly successful tour. In the one Test match he took thirteen wickets for 91 runs. On his return from South Africa, he was eligible to play for Gloucestershire, and he appeared for them as an amateur.

Although he played several good innings for the western county, Ferris could never recapture the bowling form that he had shown for Australia, and in 1895 he returned to his native country. He appeared for South Australia and for New South Wales, but the skill had deserted him forever. He died of enteric fever while serving with the Imperial Light Horse in the Boer War.

Also playing his one Test match for England in the game at Cape Town in March 1892 was W.L. Murdoch, who had been as dominant a cricketer in Australia as W.G. Grace had been in England. He toured England with five Australian sides between 1878 and 1890 and was captain of four of those sides. He had seemed to fade from the game after his marriage in 1884, but he returned to England as captain of the 1890 side after which he was dropped from the Australian side on the grounds that, at 36, he was too old. His response was to emigrate to England, settle in Sussex and captain the county from 1893 until 1899.

There was no hostility towards Ferris and Murdoch playing in England. They were amateurs, gentlemen pursuing their sporting interests among other gentlemen. They were not specifically imported to strengthen a particular county at the expense of home-bred talent although, arguably, this is what had been done in the case of Ferris even though he played as an amateur.

The attitude that was adopted to Murdoch was the same as that which was applied to Dr Leslie Poidevin who assisted Lancashire from 1904 to 1908. Poidevin won a fine reputation as a batsman with New South Wales, but, an arts graduate from Sydney University, he went to Edinburgh University to study medicine and qualified to play for Lancashire. It was considered right that he should be able to continue to play first-class cricket while resident in this country.

Poidevin, a noted sportsman, played Davis Cup tennis and later became a prominent administrator of cricket in Australia and a writer on the game.

There were some misgivings, however, as to the increasing number of importations well before Poidevin arrived. F.R. Spofforth, Australia's first demon fast bowler, retired from Australian cricket in 1887 and settled in England where he eventually became a director of the Star Tea Company. He played for Derbyshire between 1889 and 1891, but Derbyshire at that time were a second-class county. When it was announced that he was buying a house in Hampstead and could qualify for Middlesex, the magazine *Cricket* registered some apprehension that this might not be in the best interests of the game if it came about. In fact, Spofforth restricted his cricket in the London area to club cricket, mainly for Wembley Park and Hampstead, whose bowling averages he topped when he was well past fifty.

The rumpus about overseas players did not break out until the turn of the century, and before then there was a clamour in favour of an Indian playing for England.

Kumar Shri Ranjitsinhji, later H.H. Shri Sir Ranjitsinhji Vibhaji, Jam Sahib of Nawanagar, went up to Trinity College, Cambridge, in the autumn of 1892. His cricket career at University was limited in its success, but he began to play for Sussex in 1895 and captured the public imagination with a style of batting that had more than a hint of the exotic.

He had learned his cricket at Rajkumar College in Rajkot, but it had been shaped in England, although his glides and touches were essentially strokes of the spirit rather than of a coaching manual. In 1895 he hit 1,775 runs with four centuries for Sussex, and his 1896 season began in an equally rich vein. The Australians were visiting England that year, and press and public expected 'Ranji' to be chosen to face them.

In 1896 Test teams were not chosen by an independent selection committee, but by the county at whose ground the match was to be played.

The first Test match was played at Lord's and the England team was selected by MCC under the chairmanship of Lord Harris, the most recent ex-President. Prince Ranjitsinhji was excluded from the side.

Harris and his committee omitted 'Ranji' because they considered that, as an Indian by birth, he was ineligible to represent

England. Harris termed him a 'bird of passage'. This proved not to be true, for 'Ranji' was to do more for English cricket than he was for his own country. Harris was anxious that a Parsee or All-Indian side should visit England, and he hoped that the Prince would captain the All-India team, but Harris's efforts between 1897 and 1904 to bring this about were fruitless.

The omission of 'Ranji' from the England team at Lord's caused an outcry. Public and press supported him strongly, arguing that he was a most popular cricketer who had developed the skills of his game in England. The exchanges were bitter, and friendships were broken.

For the second Test match, at Old Trafford, 'Ranji' was chosen, scored a brilliant century and served England and Sussex with great charm and personality over the next few years. The circumstances of an Indian playing for England had never before been considered, and when he was selected to play Ranjitsinhji insisted that the Australians be consulted to see if they had any objection. They had not, and their captain, Harry Trott, welcomed the inclusion of one who attracted large crowds.

At the time, there was no organised first-class cricket in India, and at the turn of the century, Captain Philip Trevor was to suggest that looking for cricket in India was like looking for snakes in Iceland, but there was cricket 'of sorts'. South Africa's introduction to Test cricket did not come until March 1889, and, as we have noted, there was no worry about Australians representing England against South Africa, for the only matches that were recognised as real contests were those between England and Australia.

The emigration to England of Murdoch, Ferris and Spofforth caused little stir. They were accepted into the fold. They were all mature cricketers in their mid-thirties when they arrived, and they played as amateurs. In 1898, however, two years after Ranjitsinhji's debut for England, there was a growing sense of unease about overseas players in English cricket. Sydney Pardon, the editor of *Wisden*, recorded that the presence of Trott, Roche and O'Halloran on the MCC ground staff, with the object of them qualifying for Middlesex, had aroused 'some ill feeling and dissatisfaction among the other counties'. All three were Australian.

O'Halloran had played three games for Victoria before coming to England to join the MCC ground staff, but his first-class cricket in England was limited to just nine matches for the Marylebone Club. William Roche was an off-break bowler who was able to turn the ball appreciably. He was in the Victoria side from 1894 to 1898, and his best season was his last when he took 33 wickets, including five for 77 against the English tourists. His form had been so impressive that he was advised to go to England to seek advancement and a career as a cricketer. He qualified for Middlesex and played for them in 1899 and 1900, but he had only spasmodic success. Albert Trott was a different proposition. He arrived in England as a fully-fledged Test cricketer.

Born in Melbourne in 1873, he was a heavily built man with large hands. He was a ferocious hitter of the ball and a bowler of infinite variety, capable of swerve and spin and of genuine pace. He was an outstanding fielder. In 1894-95, he was the most exciting young cricketer in Australia and troubled Stoddart's England touring team whenever he faced them. His Test match debut, at Adelaide, was sensational.

Australia batted first in oppressively hot weather. When Trott came to the wicket they were 157 for 8. Jarvis was out immediately to make it 157 for 9, but Trott and Callaway put on 81 for the last wicket. Albert Trott finished on 38 not out. England were bowled out for 124, Trott bowling three overs for nine runs. In the second Australian innings, again at number ten, he hit 72 not out, and the last two wickets realised 128 runs. Bowling virtually unchanged throughout the England second innings, he took eight for 43. He also caught Richardson off the bowling of Giffen. His figures are the best recorded on a Test debut, although both Valentine, the West Indian spinner, and Massie, the Australian medium pacer, took eight wickets in an innings in their first Tests.

In the next Test match, Albert Trott did not bowl, but he scored 85 not out. He was less successful in the final Test match which, as it transpired, was to be his last for Australia, for whom he finished with a batting average of 102.50.

His form disappointed in the following season, but he was young and everyone expected him to be chosen for the tour of England in 1896 with the side which was captained by his brother

Harry. Albert Trott was not selected, and his omission remains one of the mysteries of cricket.

By nature, he was not a man calculated to suffer an injustice without retaliation. He sought advice from the noted umpire Jim Phillips and he was encouraged to go to England to seek his cricketing fortune. He sailed with the official Australian side, settled in London and obtained a position on the MCC ground staff with a view to qualifying for Middlesex. Another brother, Fred, was also engaged at Lord's for a time and played for Middlesex second eleven, but he never reached the level of ability of Albert or Harry and became a professional in Scotland.

Albert Trott made his mark in the matches in which he played for MCC in 1896 and 1897. In his second season, he took 48 wickets at very low cost. He made his debut for Middlesex in 1898. He injured a hand in May and failed to do himself justice, but by the time his injury had healed, in August, he was in devastating form. He and J.T. Hearne proved to be an outstanding bowling combination, and Middlesex won eight of their last nine matches, climbing to second in the table. Trott passed 100 wickets, and Lord Hawke invited him to go to South Africa where two matches, since recognised as Tests, were played. Trott's two matches for England produced only 23 runs, but he took seventeen wickets at 11.64 runs each.

It was, of course, unthinkable that he should be chosen for England against Australia.

As Lord Hawke reported, 'Albert Trott had quaint ways'. He approached Hawke and asked for money in advance so that he could send it to his brother in Australia. His lordship complied with the request, but then became suspicious that the money had gone straight to the bookmakers. When Trott repeated the tactics in Johannesburg Lord Hawke said that if Trott would give him his brother's address, he would send the money straight to him. Trott never asked again.

In 1899, he scored 1,175 runs and took 239 wickets. The following season he completed the 'double' for the second and last time with 1,337 runs and 211 wickets.

There was great hostility towards Trott as an Australian playing for an English county, but as a character he had a sense of fun which made him exceedingly popular at Lord's. Lord Hawke certainly had a soft spot for him, seeing him as one of the best all-round cricketers in the world, 'full of drollery and too apt to take his batting lightly'. Trott enjoyed a drink, and when it came to temptation he 'resisted none'.

That he excited public interest as a controversial character can been seen from the fact that he was one of the first cricketers to be wooed to lend his name to a weekly newspaper column although, as his colleagues noted, he was not a literary genius. His articles brought him into conflict with MCC on one occasion when, under his name, appeared the comment that the arrangements for a match at Lord's were scandalous because 'the beer gave out at lunch time'. When called before Francis Lacey, the secretary of MCC, Trott said, truthfully, that he had not written the piece and had not seen it. He was warned to be more careful in future about what his 'ghost' wrote, for the statement was incorrect in any case.

The antagonism towards the importation of an Australian cricketer erupted in the strangest ways. One story tells how 'Alberto', as he was known, and some of his Middlesex colleagues went to a barber's shop one day when on tour. With Trott in the chair being shaved, the conversation turned to cricket. The barber was unaware of the identity of his customers and suddenly gave vent to his feelings on the folly of Australians being allowed to play in county cricket. He added that he knew what he would do if he ever had Albert Trott in his chair beneath his razor.

Forty years on, the passions about Trott and Middlesex still burned, for E.H.D. Sewell, who had played against him, could write that Trott 'had no more right to play for Middlesex at cricket than Stalin has to lead the Guards Brigade into action', a somewhat bizarre comparison, but the intensity of feeling is apparent.

In reactions to Trott were mingled the elements that were to perpetuate the debate on overseas players in English cricket. On the one hand it was felt that he should not have been playing for a county for whom he had no true allegiance or qualification; on the other it was realised that he was a fine cricketer and a great entertainer to whom the crowds responded with warmth.

C. B. Fry regarded Trott the bowler as 'the most original, inventive and enterprising performer with the ball at present engaged in first-class cricket'. Warner spoke of him as having a wonderfully fast, straight yorker, and his 626 wickets in three years is testimony to his quality as a bowler. It was as a batsman, however, that Trott made his most memorable achievement.

He was a batsman of enormous popular appeal, and although his career at Lord's was brief, no player was ever better liked. The mighty year was 1899. At the beginning of May, he played for MCC against Sussex and hit a ball from Fred Tate so powerfully that it struck the MCC coat-of-arms which crowns the highest pinnacle on the top of the towers of the pavilion. The ball hit the emblem and bounced back into the seats. In the second innings he scored 69 in forty minutes, and it was obvious that he had become very conscious of hitting the ball into the pavilion.

Some weeks later, he played a magnificent innings of 203 against Yorkshire. He began quietly, playing himself in before lunch, but in the afternoon session he launched a violent attack on the bowling, and at one time he hit 137 out of 181 in 90 minutes.

The great event came on the last day of July when he was playing for MCC against the Australian tourists. The *Daily Telegraph* account gives the details of the matter.

'Though he did not stay very long – scarcely more than 45 minutes – Trott once he started was extremely busy. His score of 41 was in itself nothing out of the common, but he made some truly wonderful drives. He first hit Trumble over the ring at long-off, and then lifted a ball on to the top balcony of the pavilion. This caused Noble to go on, a change which as it happened brought Trott's innings to a close. Before he got the wicket, however, Noble had to suffer. Surpassing his previous efforts, Trott made a mighty hit, which cleared the pavilion roof, struck the chimney, and fell behind the building. Possibly he was a little too much elated by his success and the applause, but anyhow this great drive was the end of him. Almost directly afterwards he skied the ball to third man and was out to the easiest of catches.'

Trott is the only man to have cleared the pavilion at Lord's with a hit. The ball hit the tennis courts at the back, and Trott only got four for it, for in those days the ball had to go out of the ground for the batsman to be awarded six.

There are those who feel that Trott's famous hit was his undoing as a batsman. Using a very heavy bat, he spent the rest of his career trying to repeat the blow, to the detriment of his batting. Lord Hawke suggested that 'towards the end, he degraded his magnificent hitting powers into blind swiping'. Certainly his batting suffered from a lack of discretion, and his aggregate fell year by year.

From 1903 onwards, a year that Middlesex won the title, his powers were on the wane, and by 1905 they had declined to such an extent that *Wisden* could lament, 'Trott went from bad to worse. We cannot help thinking that he would be all the better for a little hard training during the winter and spring.' That was not Trott's way. Even at the height of his form, Gregor MacGregor had said to him, 'If you had a head instead of a turnip, Alberto, you'd be the best bowler in the world.'

He had become a shadow of his former self, but in his benefit match, at Whitsun, 1907, he showed one last flash of greatness. Middlesex's opponents were Somerset, who needed 246 to win on the last day. Trott entered the attack and dismissed Lewis, Poyntz, Woods and Robson with successive balls. He then finished the innings by performing the 'hat-trick', his victims being Mordaunt, Wickham and Bailey. A hat-trick twice in the same innings was an unprecedented feat. Trott's figures were seven for 20, and he remarked that he had bowled himself into the workhouse, although this is hardly the case as the remarkable bowling occurred on the last afternoon of the match.

He last played for Middlesex in 1910, after which he became a county umpire. His health deteriorated badly, and he was forced to give up early in 1914. He found the monotony of life in hospital intolerable and discharged himself. The nursing staff attempted to dissuade him, but he was adamant. Three days after returning to his lodgings, he shot himself. He left his worldly goods – his wardrobe and four pounds – to his landlady.

Before Trott ceased to play for Middlesex he had been joined on the staff by another Australian, Frank Tarrant. Indeed, no county has so eagerly enlisted the services of overseas players as the Metropolitan Club, a fact which prompted Neville Cardus to remark that whereas other counties relied on birth or residence for qualification, Middlesex appeared to qualify players by means of some mystical ceremony on Paddington Station.

If, in signing Trott, Middlesex were the first to encourage the recruitment of an overseas player in an effort to strengthen a side, others were quick to follow. There was great concern in 1902 when, following the Australian tour which had shown the glories of Victor Trumper to an admiring English public, overtures were made to the great batsman, 'stylish in the highest sense', to play for an English county.

The news had first broken in the *Liverpool Echo*, where an anonymous reporter had stated that Lancashire would be engaging the services of a cricketer who was of the highest quality in every department of the game. It was generally assumed that the player in question was Warwick Armstrong, but, as the *Daily Mail* pointed out some weeks later, the news was premature. It was to Victor Trumper that the approach had been made. It was also suggested that Surrey were vying with Lancashire for Trumper's services and that he could well be playing at The Oval in 1905.

The news had a shattering effect on the cricket public. It was not simply that Trumper, the hero of Australia, could be wearing the Red Rose of Lancashire, but that he would play as a professional. For one of the brightest jewels of the Golden Age, this was seen as something of a profanity. It was pointed out, however, that the South African all-rounder C.B. Llewellyn had qualified for Hampshire and played as a professional with all the dignity and integrity that is associated with the game. Llewellyn played Test cricket for South Africa in 1896 and 1899, and he was named in the England squad in 1902, but he did not appear in the final eleven.

When it was realised that a lack of financial security might be the reason for Trumper's flirtation with Lancashire, or Surrey, Joe Darling, the Australian captain, offered him a post in his sports business in Adelaide. Horrified at the prospect of losing their greatest joy, Sydney rallied to the cause, and Trumper's position in the probate office was substantiated. He later set up his own sports shop, but he had little interest in money, was naïve in business and generous to a fault, so that one doubts if Lancashire could have persuaded him to play in England.

Frank Tarrant needed no persuading. He first played for Victoria in 1898-99, when he was eighteen, and it was Pelham Warner who was instrumental in bringing him to Middlesex. When Warner was in Australia in 1902-03, he learned that Tarrant 'was anxious to make his cricket career in England'. Negotiations were begun with the Middlesex Club, and Tarrant arrived in England to begin the necessary two years' residential qualification.

In his first season, 1905, Tarrant did nothing out of the ordinary, but thereafter he could be considered on a par with George Hirst as the best all-rounder in the world. He was a studious batsman, but as he gained confidence and experience in England, he progressed from extreme caution to enterprise and hard-driving. He batted right-handed, but he bowled slow left-arm and spun the ball prodigiously. He completed the 'double' every year from 1907 to 1914. Only Hirst and Tate have comparable records of eight 'doubles' in succession.

Warner's assessment of Tarrant was fulsome in its praise. 'He was on the MCC staff, was an automatic choice for the Players, and was good enough for any England Eleven of his time. But he was a sort of "No Man's Land-er", for the rules of qualification were then strict, perhaps too strict according to modern ideas, and he could not play for England or Australia, though he was good enough for a World Eleven. I think the regulations were a bit too severe, for he had not played for Victoria in a first-class state match, though he had played for Victoria against Tasmania, which was not then in the Sheffield Shield competition.'

One would not quarrel with Warner's opinion of Tarrant's abilities, but for the rest he is guilty of some half-truths.

Tarrant had been employed as a ground bowler at Melbourne where he earned thirty shillings a week. He wanted to make his livelihood from cricket, and England was the only place where that ambition could be fulfilled. He arrived here unknown and unheralded, but there was bitter criticism when he first appeared for Middlesex, and the whole argument over 'colonial importations' raged furiously. Tarrant was, however, a discreet man. He was an intelligent and diligent professional, careful to offend nobody and anxious to violate no traditions.

Harry Lee told of how the Middlesex professionals had to be at breakfast by nine o'clock sharp, for the senior man, J.T. Hearne, would preside over the dining table at that hour. One morning, Lee arrived in the dining-room shortly before nine to find Hearne looking impatiently at his watch and asking, 'Where's Frank Tarrant this morning?' Lee rushed upstairs and found Tarrant still in bed. When told that Hearne was looking for him he got up, washed, shaved and dressed quickly and was down at breakfast within three minutes for fear of offending Hearne, to whom he was second-in-command, and violating an accepted code of behaviour. Tarrant's attitude contrasts sharply with that of a young Australian who played for Hampshire in 1980.

For all his tact, it was Tarrant who was responsible for bringing about a change in the rules of qualification following his highly successful season of 1907. *Wisden* named him as one of the Five Cricketers of the Year in 1908 and remarked that he had done well for Victoria when he had returned to Australia at the end of the season. Indeed, he had. He scored 65 and 81 in his first match, against A.O. Jones's England touring team, and followed this with 105 against South Australia and 79 and 206 against New South Wales, so helping Victoria to win the Sheffield Shield. He also hit 159 for a Victorian XI against MCC and played for An Australian XI against the tourists. This caused an outcry, was Tarrant a Middlesex player or a Victoria player? It was argued that he could not be both, and the rules were amended accordingly.

1. A cricketer may not play for more than one county within the calendar year; the penalty for infringement of this rule to be disqualification for two years. A British Colony, Dependency, or State shall, for the purpose of this rule, be regarded as a county.
2. A cricketer is always eligible to play for the county of his birth.
3. A cricketer is qualified to play for any county in which he has resided for the previous 24 months and is residing but:
   (a) The mere acquiring or hiring of a tenement, unless used as a bona fide home, does not constitute *residence*.
   (b) The occupation of a tenement during the cricket season only does not constitute *residence*.

Tarrant was not to play for Victoria again until after the First World War. His success for Middlesex continued unabated. In 1909, against Gloucestershire, he took seven for 18, opened the innings and carried his bat for 55, and then he took six for 49 as his side won by an innings. In 1914, at Leyton, Middlesex were put in to bat by Essex on a damp wicket. They declared at 464 for 1, Tarrant having hit 250 not out in five hours, twenty minutes.

He did the 'hat-trick' five times in first-class cricket, and in India, in 1918-19, he hit 182 not out and took all ten wickets for 90 when playing for the Maharaj of Cooch Behar's XI against Lord Willington's XI at Poona. Tarrant had gone to work in India shortly after the war broke out, and 1914 was to be his last season for Middlesex.

Frank Tarrant was an enthusiastic cricketer, and he was a good businessman. In 1924-25, he reappeared for Victoria and bowled and batted with enough success to suggest that he would not be out of place in the Australian side even at the age of 44. The next season he played only one match and then dropped out of first-class cricket.

His main interest at this time was buying and selling thoroughbreds in India and Australia. As in his cricket, so in his connection with the turf, he was highly successful, and he died a wealthy man.

Pelham Warner was responsible not only for bringing Tarrant to England, but also for encouraging John Dwyer, who had played no first-class cricket in Australia before coming to England in 1904. He was on the MCC ground staff, played club cricket in Brighton and qualified for Sussex. He was a useful fast-medium-pace bowler, but he is probably best remembered for being the grandson of Michael Dwyer, who was transported to Australia after the Irish rebellion of 1798.

John Cuffe had the advantage of one game for New South Wales before qualifying for Worcestershire by residence and serving them well as an all-rounder until the outbreak of war. He later played in the Lancashire League and became a first-class umpire.

While Warner was the broker responsible for bringing Tarrant and Dwyer to England, Archie MacLaren was directly influential in obtaining Alexander Kermode for Lancashire. On the insistence of Monty Noble, the great Australian all-rounder, Kermode had been picked to play for New South Wales in two matches in 1901-02. One of these matches was against MacLaren's touring side, and the Lancashire captain was so impressed with the tall, ungainly, medium-pace bowler that he induced Kermode to come to England to qualify for Lancashire.

During his period of qualification he played for Enfield in the Lancashire League, and he is believed to be the first Australian to appear in the league. He played for Lancashire from 1904 to 1906, took 113 wickets in 1905, but never reached the heights that had been expected. He later returned to the Lancashire League to play for Bacup, and after the First World War went back to Australia and played grade cricket.

Lancashire's importation of Kermode was severely criticised, and the example of Yorkshire and Nottinghamshire relying upon native talent was urged 'as desirable to be copied by all counties'. In response to the judgements that were passed upon them, Lancashire cited Trott and Middlesex as a precedent, and the critics were aware that the dyke had been breached.

The deepest concern was felt when Surrey registered Alan Marshal. His qualification was brought about by means of residence, but the way in which that qualification was achieved troubled many people in the cricket world.

Alan Marshal was born in Queensland and learned his cricket when his family moved to Brisbane. He came under the influence of Australian Test players McDonnell, Boyle and Jones, and he joined the Paddington Club in Sydney in order to further his cricket. He returned to Brisbane in 1903-04, and he was selected for the state side, but Queensland was not in the Sheffield Shield at that time, and opportunities were limited.

Marshal had become passionately devoted to cricket, and he sailed to England to qualify for Surrey and earn his living by playing the game he loved.

He was unquestionably a magnificent prospect. He was one of the greatest batsmen Queensland has ever produced, a splendid hitter of the ball. He was also an outstanding fielder and a bowler capable of both pace and spin. The manner of his qualifying for Surrey, however, caused severe criticism. He fulfilled the necessary two years' residence, but while he was doing this it was common knowledge that Surrey were paying him a winter allowance. This was interpreted as a poaching. In effect, Surrey had bribed him to come to England and were buying the services of an overseas player. The concern was that the residential and birth qualifications which had given the first-class game in England stability for over a quarter of a century were being undermined by those counties who had sufficient wealth, a wealth which gave them power.

Marshal was able to play for W.G. Grace's London County side while he was qualifying for Surrey, although by 1905 the club had ceased to play first-class fixtures. He excited by his tremendous powers of hitting, and he is reported to have scored 4,350 runs, with fourteen centuries, in minor matches in 1906. The following year was his first for Surrey and was something of a disappointment. So much had been expected of him, but the argument over his eligibility and the personal criticism to which he was subjected in some quarters obviously affected him. Like some who were to come after him, he was guilty of trying too hard to justify himself.

The 1908 season was a triumph for Marshal. He hit 1884 runs for Surrey, and *Wisden* selected him as one of the Five Cricketers of the Year. Sydney Pardon was ecstatic about his powers of hitting. 'Some of his hits in the matches against Middlesex and Kent at The Oval in August were, I think, beyond the capacity of any other batsman now playing in first-class cricket.' At 6' 3", he had an immense advantage in height and reach, but nothing should detract from outstanding knocks.

His 176 against Worcestershire came in 200 minutes, and his 167 against Kent saw him outshine Jack Hobbs in a third-wicket stand of 239. As he also bowled well enough to take 55 wickets, the future seemed bright indeed.

The next year, however, things began to go wrong. The Surrey Committee offered no explanation for suspending him for a time at the height of the season. A year later, after five matches in which he did next to nothing, Marshal had his contract terminated. The reasons were never fully explained, but the terms 'insubordination' and 'gross irregularities' were most commonly used. There were suggestions that some of the irregularities concerned finance.

It was an unhappy time for Surrey. They had trouble with some of their professionals, and J.N. Crawford, a most gifted young amateur all-rounder, left the Club after a quarrel. He had refused to captain the County against the Australian tourists because certain professionals had been left out of the team. The Surrey Committee demanded an apology, which Crawford refused to give, and he accepted a teaching post in Australia where he played Sheffield Shield cricket. He returned to England after the First World War and assisted Surrey for two more seasons, the quarrel having been patched up.

The quarrel with Marshal was never patched up, and he returned to Australia, where he regained his place in the Queensland side, but in spite of a century for an Australian xi against the South Africans in the 1910-11 season, he was never given the opportunity to display his talents at the highest level.

When war broke out, he joined the Australian Imperial Forces, served in Gallipoli, and died of enteric fever in a military hospital in Malta in July 1915. He was 32, and, as *Wisden* commented, 'He was a cricketer of unfulfilled promise. He had it in him to be great, but somehow he missed the position that at one time seemed to be within his reach.' He holds a significant position in cricket history, however, for the rumpus that he caused when he was engaged by Surrey.

The antagonism that was directed at Marshal, particularly in his first season with Surrey, was, in a sense, not personal, but part of an anger born of a sudden realisation that the number of importations into county cricket was growing annually. It must be emphasised that the hostility was directed towards those who were signed as professionals, who were seen to be depriving a home-bred player of his livelihood.

Sammy Woods, who assisted the Australian side in England in 1888 and later played for Lord Hawke's England side in South Africa, came to England in 1894, went to Brighton College and Cambridge and was secretary of Somerset until 1923. Woods, a great all-round sportsman, appeared for the Gentlemen several times and, although Australian by birth, he was so long in Somerset that he was accepted as a West Country cricketer.

Sydney Gordon Smith was another whose background and social status gave him immunity from being considered as an importation. He was born in Trinidad and toured England with H.B.G. Austin's side in 1906. A most able left-handed all-rounder, Smith made a good impression on the tour 'and it was soon arranged that he should stay in England and qualify for Northamptonshire'. He played against the Philadelphians in 1908 and was qualified to play in the county championship in 1909 when he did the 'double' and became the first Northamptonshire cricketer to score a thousand runs in a season. The following season he established another record for the county with an innings of 204 against Gloucestershire, and he completed the 'double' again in 1913 and 1914, by which time he had become Northamptonshire's captain and brought about a considerable change in their fortunes. He often played for the Gentlemen and was named as one of *Wisden*'s Five Cricketers of the Year.

Smith was an amateur, and he was white. Charles Ollivierre qualified for Derbyshire as a professional, and he was black. He came to England with the West Indian side of 1900 and made a fine impression as a batsman although the team did not play first-class matches. He stayed in England and qualified for Derbyshire, for whom he played from 1902 until 1907, when he was forced to retire from first-class cricket because of eye trouble.

Ollivierre scored well for his adopted county and played a memorable innings against Essex in 1904. This was the occasion at Chesterfield when, with Perrin scoring 343 not out, Essex reached 597 in their first innings. Derbyshire responded with 548, of which Ollivierre made 229. Essex were bowled out for 97 in their second innings, and Derbyshire went on to win by nine wickets. In 1931, in his book *Cricket Up-To-Date*, E.H.D. Sewell, who played in the match, gave this account of the closing stages of the game:

'The interest in this absorbingly interesting game had not by any means yet evaporated. It had happened that in their first innings a man of colour, C.A. Ollivierre – and except Ranji and Trumper of deathless renown, no player had better wrists than this coal-black batsman – had made 229. He was soon well on his way to the then rare feat – there were bowlers and captains in those days – of a hundred in both innings of a match. Early on he was joined by the late Bill Storer, a man who believed in England for the English and was not enamoured of importations, especially those of ebony hue. Storer soon dug himself in and proceeded to make tracks for talent money. As "time" and the inevitable result drew near we had the not unamusing spectacle of one batsman trying to bag the bowling in order to get his second hundred, and the other anxious to secure the strike because of the sovereign now dangling so close that its glitter could almost be seen; while both naturally wanted to win the game. In the end Storer missed talent by two runs and the black his hundred by eight, but Derbyshire got home all right.'

One shudders to think what the reaction would be to such an account and such a choice of words today, but Sewell was among the leading cricket writers for over forty years, and none would have challenged his assertion that Bill Storer, who played for Derbyshire for eighteen years, was not happy to be playing alongside an 'importation', particularly one from the Caribbean.

The conflict would not subside. In 1909, Warren Bardsley, having completed a most successful tour of England with the Australian side, received overtures from leading English counties. C.E. Green was incensed and wrote to *The Times*, a more significant act then than it is today. Green saw the importation of overseas cricketers as prejudicing the real character and traditions of county cricket and the spirit of comradeship which should exist in this type of cricket.

'Real county cricket is the backbone of our English cricket, and every possible endeavour should be made to keep this as genuine and real as it is possible and to prevent it ever becoming merely a gate money business affair, which the engaging of outside 'star' players to strengthen a county side must ultimately cause it to be'.

Green had vision, and he took up his pen again when Frank Tarrant was named in the England side against the Rest in the Test Trial at Lord's, at the end of June 1911. The match was arranged to help the selectors to choose the side to visit Australia under Warner and to consider players for the Triangular Tournament in England the following summer.

'Tarrant was born and bred in Australia, where he learnt his cricket, and it will be remembered that after he qualified for Middlesex he went back to Australia, where he played for Victoria and in other matches against the last English team visiting that country, and I have reason to believe he was willing, if selected, to play for Australia in the Test matches. This position was, however, so anomalous that it was decided at headquarters that a telegram should be sent to Tarrant informing him that if he continued to play for an Australian State he would forfeit his county qualification for Middlesex. Even if by any recently amended rules Tarrant might now technically be qualified to play for England, surely it is against the spirit of international cricket that England should be represented by a player born and bred in Australia.'

Tarrant was now technically qualified to play for England under the rules discussed at the Imperial Conference on 15 June 1909, when the staging of the Triangular Tournament between England, South Africa and Australia was approved. That technicality allowed that Tarrant's length of residence in Middlesex and his qualification for that county made him eligible for England. He did well in the Test Trial, but he was never selected for an England side, the selectors feeling it better not to press the claims of the 'technicality' and cause an angry debate.

Soon the whole debate was overtaken by other events. In August 1914, the First World War broke out, and in the slaughter that followed, the question of residential and birth qualification seemed a trivial one. By the end of the war moods and attitudes had undergone a radical change, and C.E. Green, who had fought a balanced and visionary campaign in the light of his beliefs, was dead.

PART 2
Between the Acts

When first-class cricket resumed in 1919 the professional importations had disappeared. There were several amateurs playing for counties in the 1920s who had been born overseas, but most of them were following courses of study in England. Somerset enlisted the occasional help of the Oxford pair, Blaikie and Wharton, one South African, the other born in the West Indies, and for some years they also included Manek Bajana, who had come to England with the All-India team in 1911, but, in fact, never played first-class cricket in India. Sydney Maartensz, from Ceylon, was a useful wicket-keeper for Hampshire, and Louis Serrurier, at Oxford, played a few games for Worcestershire before returning to South Africa to represent Western Province, and later Transvaal, in the Currie Cup.

Tom Lowry went with MacLaren's side to Australia and New Zealand in 1922-23, and later captained Somerset and Cambridge University before returning to his native land, New Zealand, and leading them in most able fashion. Bettington and Gunasekera were medical men from Australia and Ceylon who played for Middlesex, while another Australian, Hopkins, also a doctor, played for Worcestershire.

These amateurs from abroad were welcomed, even encouraged by the establishment, and there were suggestions that it should be made easier for them to be registered for a county. Pelham Warner, born in the West Indies, editor of the newly founded magazine *The Cricketer*, was strong in his support for the overseas amateur.

'We hope that the question of county qualification will be thoroughly gone into this winter, and that some scheme of registration will be brought in. It is not suggested that a man should

34

be bought and sold, as is done in professional football, but what we want to do is to obtain as many amateurs as we can to play county cricket. The professional cricketer is a splendid fellow. He is loyal and steady, the best of companions on a tour, and always ready to oblige, but the amateur must be encouraged. At present the rules governing county qualification are too rigid. We are a great Empire, and a man's birthplace is an accident. Take the cases of a boy born in India, or South Africa, or the West Indies. His father, perhaps, is a professional man – a barrister, let us say, in India or South Africa. He sends his boy home to England at the age of eight or nine to a preparatory school. The boy then goes to a public school, then to a University; he 'eats his dinners' at the Temple, or joins a business house, intending to return to the country of his birth. He becomes a fine cricketer at school or University, but as he spends his holidays and vacations with friends and relations in various parts of the country, his parents being resident abroad, he possesses no county qualification.

'We should therefore like to see a man in such a position register for a county. There would, of course, have to be certain safeguards to counter any undue influence, the details of which could be easily worked out; but we believe that some such scheme would be of great benefit to first-class cricket. As things are at present we take too parochial a view of our cricket.'

Warner's opinion, which was expressed at the beginning of August 1921, was supported by correspondents, one of whom suggested that a man should be eligible to play for the county of his father's birth. Warner's liberalism on qualification did not extend to the professional, even though he had been responsible for bringing Tarrant and Dwyer to England, and it was with horror seven weeks later that, in commenting on E.A. McDonald, 'the best fast bowler on our wickets that Australia has ever sent us', he hoped 'sincerely that he is not going to stay in this country and play for a League club, as is strongly rumoured'.

The rumour proved to be founded on fact, and in reviewing the Lancashire League season for *The Cricketer* in the Winter Annual, 1921-22, G.A. Brooking was strong in his condemnation.

'With regard to the action of the Nelson Club in engaging E.A. McDonald as their professional for three years, I am in total disagreement. Offering terms to an English professional, and an Australian on tour in this country, are two different things. Australia have only a limited number of players to draw on, and there is such a thing as thinking Imperially.

'If three other clubs had tempted Gregory, Macartney, and Bardsley, it would have been very unfair to Australia. Of course, from the viewpoint of the Nelson club, it is a successful business transaction, but to those who really love the game of fair play, it is a matter of great regret, as it is nothing less than taking from the Commonwealth the best fast bowler in the world.'

Mr Brooking's concern for Australia was unnecessary. They had just beaten England in eight successive Tests, and they were to trounce England again three years later, without the help of McDonald.

The major leagues came into existence in the last decade of the nineteenth century, and professionalism was fashionable from the turn of the century. At first, the professional's main duty was to serve the club as net organiser and groundsman. Mainly, professionals were retired county players, and although the crowds were attracted by their prowess, they batted and bowled only when necessary, allowing those whom they coached and encouraged to take the major part in the Saturday afternoon game.

After the First World War there was a change in attitude as clubs contended to engage the best possible players. The great S.F. Barnes had spent most of his career in league cricket, and McDonald was the first cricketer of international standing to be wooed to the Lancashire League after the war. The cotton trade was in a period of boom, and wealthy traders were prepared to subsidise clubs who signed leading players. The professional was now the star performer, the attractor of large crowds, rather than the faithful, hard-working club servant. In persuading McDonald to sign for them, Nelson achieved the first great scoop by a northern league club. He put Nelson on the map, and people flocked to see him.

Edgar Arthur McDonald was born in Tasmania, for whom he first played in 1909-10 before his eighteenth birthday. After two seasons he moved to Victoria, where he was regarded primarily as a batsman, but shortly before the outbreak of war, he began to display the qualities of an outstanding fast bowler. He was tall, broad shouldered and approached the wicket with a high, balanced, smooth fifteen-pace run. There was no strain, no forced endeavour in the delivery. He had the classical economic action as he glided over the ground, and there are those who believe that the game has never seen a faster bowler. He could move the ball either way and vary his pace, but he needed to be spurred by an occasion.

He did not play Test cricket until 1920-21, when he appeared in the last three tests against J.W.H.T. Douglas's side. He took only six wickets at a high cost, but it was obvious from the number of times that he beat the bat that here was one of the great fast bowlers.

That view was confirmed on the 1921 tour to England, when he took 150 wickets and formed a lethal opening bowling partnership with Gregory. In the Tests, McDonald took 27 wickets, and he and Gregory, on the strength of that one series, have been placed on a par with Lindwall and Miller, Lillee and Thomson, and Tyson and Statham.

He went to South Africa in 1921-22, played in the three Tests, and that, at the age of thirty, was the end of his international career, for after some fine Sheffield Shield performances, he joined Nelson for the 1922 Lancashire League season.

His beginning was inauspicious. Against Bacup 'he failed to contribute to his side's total of 56, and had an analysis of 18 overs, 6 maidens, 46 runs, and 3 wickets during the Bacup innings of 151 for six wickets.'

From then on, however, McDonald was a success. He took 99 wickets and scored 366 runs, and at times he bowled with Cecil Parkin, the Lancashire and England player. Nelson finished eighth, but they did well financially, 'owing to the magnetic power of McDonald'. The match of the season, according to Brooking, was at Church on 21 June, when the home side, being without a professional, engaged the veteran S.F. Barnes. A huge crowd turned out to see the dual between the two great players. McDonald took seven for 29, though not bowling at his fastest, and Church were out for 59. Barnes then rendered Nelson helpless as he took six for 19 and shot the visitors out for 44. 'Church batted a second time, and only made 38, McDonald, not to be outdone, bowled at a great speed, and splendid length, taking five wickets for but 7 runs!'

In 1923, he was even more successful, taking 112 wickets at 6.67 runs each, including all ten wickets for 18 runs against Burnley. He was also Nelson's leading batsman, and the club climbed to third in the league.

At this time there was no indication that he would join Lancashire, although hints were strong that he would be qualified to play for them after the completion of two years' residence in May 1924. The *Daily News* reported: 'E.A. McDonald, the Australian fast bowler, who created so much havoc among English wickets in 1921, was at one period said to be qualifying for Lancashire. In the autumn of 1923, however, the Australian then assisting Nelson in the Lancashire League, stated definitely that he had no desire to play county cricket.'

In *The Cricketer*'s pre-season review of county prospects, in spring 1924, the name of McDonald was not mentioned in the Lancashire section. There were, however, two significant events which prompted Lancashire to woo McDonald more earnestly. One was the failure of Hall, the South African Test player who was born in Bolton and subsequently returned to South Africa; the other was the death of Frank O'Keefe.

O'Keefe was a fine batsman, outstanding fielder and useful off-break bowler. He had made a tremendous impression in two seasons for New South Wales, and his career record in first-class cricket in Australia is 926 runs, average 71.23. He decided to pursue a cricket future in the Lancashire League and to qualify for Lancashire. He played for Church in 1922 and 1923 and was due to take a place in the county side in June 1923, when his residential qualification would be completed. Sadly, his health weakened by the damper English weather, he died of peritonitis three months before his qualification date.

Lancashire were ambitious, as is shown by their courting of Hall and O'Keefe, and it is likely that they were interested in McDonald from the moment he signed for Nelson. The Australian was persuaded to assist Lancashire, but it is doubtful if he needed much persuading. He was a man who needed to be tested by the best. He always bowled better against the likes of Hobbs, Sutcliffe and Hammond than he did against a number ten or eleven. He responded to a challenge, and he needed it to bring out the best in him. One cannot think that he would have been satisfied with league cricket for the rest of his life, although he was a somewhat detached and taciturn man and his moods and thoughts were hard to determine.

His first appearance for Lancashire was against Kent at Old Trafford on 28, 29 and 30 May. The game was drawn, and McDonald took six for 73 in Kent's first innings. He was still under contract to Nelson and could only assist Lancashire in mid-week fixtures. Nelson finished second in the Lancashire League, and McDonald took 99 wickets, more than any other bowler in the League, and was Nelson's leading run-getter. For Lancashire, he took 62 wickets, and the county finished fourth in the championship.

Lancashire had last won the championship in 1904, but they had been challenging strongly in the seasons since the war. As we have said, they were ambitious, and McDonald provided the extra dimension that they needed to become a championship-winning side. Lancashire's ambition was heightened by the fact that, since 1921, Yorkshire had been the dominant county, and Yorkshire won the title again in 1925 when Lancashire were third and McDonald, in his first full season, took 205 first-class wickets.

Now began the golden age of Lancashire cricket as Ted McDonald swept all before him. In the seasons 1926, 1927 and 1928, he took 484 wickets in the county championship, and Lancashire won the title three years in succession. His presence attracted large crowds – 'there had never been so many people on the Aigburth ground', 'at Nelson there were 10,000 people on the Saturday'. After the first championship season Lancashire were in a prosperous position, for even after making substantial ground improvements, they showed a net profit of £10,000.

None could deny either the appeal or the quality of McDonald as a fast bowler. *Wisden* was unstinting in its praise year after year. 'It was McDonald more than any other player in the eleven who won the matches at the season's end, and so took advantage of those chances which came Lancashire's way.' 'McDonald was rarely as fast as he was in 1921. None the less, he was far faster than the average English fast bowler. His temperament seemed to thrive on any situation which gave his side a sporting chance; he won more than one game against time in a manner that did credit both to his imagination and opportunism. He is a bowler of varying moods – and varying paces. But, at a pinch, he can achieve true greatness, both of technique and temperament.'

In 1927, a wet summer, he resorted to bowling off-breaks round the wicket on occasions and he was dreadfully served by his fielders, but he still accomplished great work although, at times, he 'pitched very short and when he did so, much exception was, in some quarters, taken to his methods'.

Parkin departed to the Lancashire League after his newspaper indiscretion and his benefit, and McDonald was left to carry the Lancashire attack, aided by Richard Tyldesley's leg-breaks. He did so manfully, seemingly unworried by the amount of work he was asked to take on. He was unquestionably the jewel in the Lancashire crown, and in 1929, he was granted the match with Middlesex at Old Trafford as his benefit. He had played only four and a half seasons with the county when the benefit was awarded.

Lancashire won the Championship again in 1930, and it is worth noting that of the seven occasions when they have won the title outright, four were achieved with McDonald in the side. They were runners-up in 1929, and in 1931, his last season when he played in only fourteen matches and was nearing forty, they finished sixth. He created the golden age of Lancashire cricket.

When Lancashire beat Kent at Old Trafford, in 1928, McDonald took fifteen for 154. Cardus deemed it one of the very greatest of bowling feats that he had seen. 'He, of course, won the match; on the flawless wicket every other bowler who took part in the game was helpless. Lockwood could not let us have seen a greater attack. Bowling of McDonald's skill and dreadful beautiful energy ennobles the game; the spark of it belongs to life immortal and it kindles imagination's fires in all men who look on. When McDonald ran to the wicket yesterday Old Trafford held its breath; you could have heard a pin drop. The greatest bowler of our day!'

McDonald returned to the Lancashire League with Bacup, and although he was not quite the force he had been in his earlier years, he could produce bursts of electrifying speed. He died in 1937 in tragic circumstances. His car was forced off the road by another car near Bolton. McDonald was unhurt and clambered out of his car and on to the roadway to try to help the other driver. He was then hit by a third car and killed.

Glorious as he was to Lancashire, McDonald's presence in county cricket was not appreciated by many other clubs. E.H.D. Sewell, as ever, was the most outspoken on the subject.

'I shall never forget being present while a certain Lancashire official attempted unsuccessfully, but in the most serious manner possible, to convince "Shrimp" Leveson-Gower that all the counties ought to be grateful to Lancashire for qualifying McDonald, because by doing so Lancashire had given their friends some much-needed practice against fast bowling! As a colossal piece of impertinence I think that argument beat anything I ever heard. However, the last has been heard of this kind of thing, because it is now impossible for a repetition of such an unfair performance as the buying of a ready-made Test match cricketer to play in cricket much of which is far below his class . . . To the detriment of county cricket, and certainly not in every case to the improvement of the kind of relations which ought to exist between our county clubs.'

Sewell's condemnation of Lancashire was unequivocal. 'Had one of the lesser and struggling counties contained a rich patron who, wishing to see his county XI sometimes in the first three, placed his cheque-book at the county club's disposal, there might have been some excuse; but, for any very large and wealthy county to descend to such methods was, and always will be, an unpardonable offence against the high and dignified example which any and all of the 'Big Six' county clubs are expected to set to the others.'

Sewell was adamant that the acquisition by a county of a Test cricketer from overseas could not now be repeated because all had agreed to be governed by Rule XI, which meant that, in future, Lancashire would have to obtain permission from Victoria before they invited another McDonald to qualify for them. But

Sewell's optimism had too weak a foundation. England was the only country where a man could earn a living by playing cricket, and the leagues still offered a gateway to the county game.

McDonald's time in England established three things that were to have wider repercussions in the years to come: a county side could buy success by importing a player of outstanding ability, particularly a bowler; a cricketer of international renown attracted large crowds; the Lancashire League could provide a good source of income for an overseas professional and could also provide him with a very good standard of cricket, well supported, while he was qualifying for an English county.

The first of these was not to be exploited until nearly forty years later; the boom in the Lancashire League was to date from the time of McDonald.

Learie Nicholas Constantine first came to England with the West Indian side of 1923. On that tour he was noted almost exclusively for his fielding. A highly intelligent and thinking man, he learned much on that tour which was to influence the course of the rest of his life. He recognised that only his cricketing ability could lead him to the kind of life he wanted and that any self-respecting human being should expect. As C.L.R. James wrote in his memorable passage on Constantine in *Beyond a Boundary*, 'He revolted against the revolting contrast between his first-class status as a cricketer and his third-class status as a man.'

Constantine practised relentlessly, and when he came to England with the 1928 West Indian side he was an outstanding success. He did the 'double', but it was not just the achievement, but the manner of his play that captivated people. He was a fast bowler, a furious hitter and a breath-taking fielder. He was a dynamic cricketer, and crowds responded to him with enthusiasm, for he emanated a sense of adventure and joy.

He wished to study Law, and that was made possible for him when he accepted an offer to join Nelson in the Lancashire League. He was a black man, and he received no approach from a county.

Constantine played for Nelson from 1929 until 1938, and during that time the club won the League on eight occasions, a feat unapproached by any other side. Moreover, with Constantine in the side, Nelson broke the ground attendance record at every ground in the League. From a 'sixpenny gate', £303 was taken at East Lancashire in 1931, £340 at Turf Moor, Burnley, in 1932, and £358 at Colne in 1935. It was the same pattern wherever Constantine and Nelson played.

In 1933 he became the first Nelson player to score a thousand runs and take a hundred wickets in a season, and in 1934 he took 10 for 10 against Accrington. It was said that towards the end of his time at Nelson he was being paid £60 a match, and when he moved to Rochdale in the Central Lancashire League in 1938 it was said that he was paid £850 for a twenty-week engagement. At that time, a county professional was paid £8 for a three-day away match and £9 if the match spread over a week-end, and from this amount he had to pay his own lodging expenses.

In 1931, when McDonald left Lancashire, Constantine was made aware that he would be unacceptable to the county club as a professional mainly because of his colour. A year later, a faction in the club again forwarded him for registration, but the signing was violently opposed, not only on account of his colour, but because he had written some uncomplimentary remarks about the dourness of Roses matches.

To followers of the game today, used to a Lancashire side that has fielded Lloyd, Engineer, Patterson, Croft and Mendis, an accusation of racial prejudice may seem nonsense, but, in 1944, Constantine, then a welfare worker with the Ministry of Labour, fought and won a case against the Imperial Hotel in London on the grounds of racial prejudice in that they had failed to 'receive and lodge him'. A year later, he received the warmest tribute from his fellow professionals when, on the withdrawal of Hassett through injury, the ten white members of the Dominions side asked that he should be captain against England.

In 1954 he was called to the Bar by the Middle Temple. In the years that followed he was a Member of Parliament in Trinidad, High Commissioner in London, the recipient of a knighthood and of a Life Peerage. Perhaps the most touching honour of all came in 1963 when he was given the Freedom of the Borough of Nelson, the town to which he felt that he owed so much and whose cricket team he had made famous.

In effect, Learie Constantine played only 119 first-class matches, eighteen of which were Tests; but for Nelson and the Lancashire League his cricket talent would have been wasted. In return, as C.L.R. James points out, 'He paved the way for that stream of Test players from the Dominions and the Colonies who for years have made their gifts familiar to hundreds of thousands who would otherwise have seen nothing or little of them. Constantine put the league on its feet financially when it was on an edge.'

Martindale, Achong, Amar Singh and Amarnath were among the Test cricketers who followed Constantine into the leagues in the years before the Second World War, and the post-war period saw Worrell, Weekes, Ramadhin, Sobers, Lindwall, Rice and a host of others. Constantine blazed a trail which others followed, and he was responsible, at least indirectly, for making it possible for many famous overseas players to come into English cricket.

One who followed him into the Lancashire League was Bill Merritt, the New Zealand leg-spinner, who played for Rishton and later moved to Dudley. Merritt joined Northamptonshire in 1939, so becoming the fourth New Zealander to enter county cricket in the years before the war.

The first was Cecil Dacre. He had excited as a batsman when playing against Archie McLaren's MCC side in 1922-23, and he was vice-captain of the New Zealand team that came to England in 1927. He batted well in the early part of the tour, and, unsolicited, he decided to remain in England at the end of the tour and to qualify for Gloucestershire, a county with which his family had connections. He was a stocky, strong batsman who was a particularly fine driver of the ball, but, exciting as he could be, he was inconsistent. He played some entertaining innings for the county from 1930 to 1936, but he lost form in his last two seasons and returned to New Zealand without ever having reached the heights that had been expected.

In qualifying for Gloucestershire after the 1927 tour, Dacre denied himself a Test career, but Ken James played in New Zealand's first eleven Test matches before deciding to qualify for Northamptonshire.

James was a wicket-keeper of the highest order. Immaculate in all that he did, he anticipated John Murray in style, and he was one who derived immense enjoyment from the game. He played for New Zealand from 1929 to 1933, after which he came to England and kept wicket for Northants from 1935 until the outbreak of war. He appeared for the RAF in matches at Lord's during the war and when he left cricket he became a publican.

It was James who recommended his friend and colleague, Merritt, to Northants. Merritt was a useful batsman as well as a spinner who had had moments of success in Test cricket where his lack of consistency restricted his appearances to six matches. He was not qualified to play for Northants until 1939, and his career for them was restricted to that season and to the season after the war, 1946.

Merritt's arrival at Northamptonshire coincided with their first victory in a first-class match for four years. At the beginning of May 1939, they beat Cambridge University by 78 runs, Merritt taking seven for 69 and five for 92, and Ken James accounting for five batsmen in the first innings.

One of New Zealand's finest batsmen, C.S. Dempster, also came into county cricket in the 1930s. He was the scorer of New Zealand's first Test century, and on the 1931 tour of England he confirmed that he was a player of the highest class by hitting 1,778 runs, average 59.26. He played ten Test matches and averaged 65.72 in his fifteen innings, so that it was a great disappointment when, in 1933, he took up a business appointment in England with Sir Julien Cahn. He assisted Leicestershire between 1935 and 1939, and, unlike James, Merritt and Dacre, he played as an amateur, captaining Leicestershire from 1936 to 1938.

Sir Julien Cahn can well be described as one of Sewell's rich patrons who put his cheque-book at the disposal of one of the lesser counties. He inherited the Nottinghamshire Furniture Company from his father, and in days when such people were scarcer than they are today, he was a millionaire. He was also a philanthropist who adored cricket. He helped Nottinghamshire in their attempts to improve the Trent Bridge ground, and he himself built two cricket grounds, the first at West Bridgford and the second at his home, Stanford Hall, near Loughborough.

From 1926 until 1939, he ran his own side and apart from the captain, Sir Julien himself, all the players were of first-class standing, with invariably three or four Test cricketers among them. Cahn was a modest cricketer, flattered even by his 70 first-class runs, average 10, and his two expensive first-class wickets. To the game, however, he was a great benefactor, and he took sides to Jamaica, Denmark, Argentina, Canada, Malaya and elsewhere to help further its cause. He was also most helpful to Midland counties, Leicestershire in particular, in encouraging overseas cricketers to come to England, employing them while they were qualifying. As well as Dempster, Crisp, the South African fast bowler, played for Cahn's side, and Crisp joined his fellow countrymen, Ahl, Martin and Cullen, at Worcestershire. More significantly, he aided four Australian cricketers and two of them were to give Leicestershire yeoman service. The four players were Mudge, Lush, Walsh and Jackson.

Harold Mudge was a delightful right-handed batsman and a leg-break bowler good enough to take six for 42 for New South Wales against G.O. Allen's MCC touring side in 1936. A year later, he joined Sir Julien Cahn's outfit. He played for Leicestershire against Oxford University in June 1937, but he showed no desire to play county cricket and returned to Australia and New South Wales in 1939-40.

John 'Ginty' Lush was a different prospect, and he remains one of the great losses to Australian Test cricket. He was a devastatingly handsome all-rounder, a ferocious and courageous hitter and a very fast, if sometimes wild, bowler. He forced his way into the New South Wales side in 1936-37 and bowled with great success. In the return match between New South Wales and MCC in February, 1937, he returned figures of six for 43 and seven for 72 as the state side won by 105 runs. He came to the wicket when Chipperfield had his jaw broken by a ball from Ken Farnes and played a brave and accomplished innings of 49. It was his first match against a touring side. It seemed certain that he would be in the Australian side for the fifth Test, but the selectors recalled Laurie Nash who had not played a first-class game all summer. Even more surprisingly, he could find no place in the Australian side to tour England in 1938, although that side was woefully weak in bowling.

Disheartened by the treatment he had received from the selectors, he was ripe for capture when approached by the former Test cricketer Alan Fairfax who, acting on behalf of Sir Julien Cahn, offered him £600 a year to join the millionaire's side. At the time, 'Ginty' Lush was earning £5 a week as a junior reporter with a Sydney newspaper and £4-10s for every Sheffield Shield appearance. Cahn's offer was one that he was unlikely to refuse, and he joined Mudge, Walsh and Jackson in playing for a man who was determined to win and who made it possible for the cricketers that he had assembled to live a life of luxury. Lush insisted that he derived more pleasure in playing for Cahn's side than the seventeen-man Australian party did from their tour of England in 1938.

He toured New Zealand with Cahn's side in 1939, but on the outbreak of war his contract was terminated and he returned to Australia. He regained his place in the New South Wales side which won the Sheffield Shield, and, in 1946-47, he captained the state against Wally Hammond's England side. He was still able to generate enough pace to cause Len Hutton a trip to hospital after he had deflected a ball into his face.

By then Lush was 34 and his first-class career had been 'lost'. Victor Jackson and Jack Walsh reshaped their first-class careers by playing for Leicestershire. Both of them came to county cricket via Sir Julien Cahn's XI.

Walsh had played no first-class cricket before signing for Cahn, but Jackson played for New South Wales in 1936-37 at the age of twenty. He was a splendid all-rounder, an off-spin bowler and middle-order batsman, and met with considerable success in his season in the Sheffield Shield. Like Mudge, Lush and Walsh, he was approached by Alan Fairfax, Sir Julien Cahn's agent, and, feeling he had little chance of being selected for the Australian Test side, he accepted the lucrative contract that was offered to him.

While playing for Cahn's side he qualified for Leicestershire and played a couple of non-championship matches for them before the war as an amateur. He returned to them in 1946 and played as a professional until 1957, when he went into the Lancashire League. Eventually, he returned to Australia and was killed when the car in which he was travelling was struck by a train on a level crossing. He had a tremendous zest for the game, and for a decade he and Jack Walsh were the backbone of Leicestershire cricket, better known in England than they were in their own country.

Jackson scored over 14,000 runs and took 930 wickets for Leicestershire, and he did the 'double' in 1955. He lived with Walsh when he first came to England, and Walsh, like Jackson, first played as an amateur.

Jack Walsh was one of the very great left-arm slow bowlers, a fact which has been obscured because he played so little in Australia and never appeared in a Test match. In three matches in 1938, he took 21 wickets for Leicestershire and, as *Wisden* commented, 'showed himself to be one of the most deadly left-arm bowlers in the country'. He had begun as a conventional finger spinner, but became fascinated by back-of-the-wrist spin and perfected this type of bowling, with a devastating 'Chinaman', to a level that few have equalled. Forty years on, Tom Pearce, the Essex captain of the years before and after the Second World War, and a Test selector, remembers him as 'one of the greatest spinners I ever played against. Tom Wade was the only Essex player of my day who could ever read him.'

He was rarely available for Leicestershire in 1939, and when war broke out, after his only two matches for New South Wales, he joined the RAAF and served in the South Pacific. In 1946, he returned to Leicestershire and joined the staff, playing for the county as a professional until he retired from first-class cricket at the end of the 1956 season. Not only did he take 1,127 wickets for Leicestershire, but he also hit 6,892 runs.

Like Albert Trott, he would have scored many more runs had he been able to curb his desire to hit every ball into the pavilion. His highest innings, against Essex in 1948, was 106, and it came in 95 minutes, with seven sixes and ten fours. He did the 'double' in 1952 and took 174 wickets in 1948, but, according to the Australian cricket historian Jack Pollard, he considered that his greatest achievement was to take 148 wickets in 1946, as he had come to Leicestershire straight from the war in Dutch New Guinea and Borneo. When he left first-class cricket he coached, for a time with Leicestershire and then in Scotland and Tasmania. He loved every minute of the games in which he played and, as an Australian, he was deeply touched to be selected for the Players against the Gentlemen at Lord's in 1947.

Leicestershire did not have the monopoly of overseas cricketers in the years before the war, for, as we have mentioned, Worcestershire had the services of the South Africans, Ahl, Martin, Crisp and Cullen, and of the Australian Frank Warne.

A member of a famous Australian cricketing family, F.B. Warne played two games for Victoria before coming to England to qualify for Worcestershire. Sometimes compared to the famous jockey Gordon Richards in stature and appearance, Warne was a solid left-handed batsman and a spin bowler who claimed the wicket of John Langridge with his first ball in county cricket. He scored a thousand runs and took 44 wickets in 1935, and he played first-class cricket in India during the winter, appearing for Europeans and coaching, which seems somehow not to have violated the rules on qualification brought in after Tarrant's appearances for Victoria. In 1936, he was taken ill and underwent an operation in June, and he was later given special permission by MCC to return home to Australia for a while as part of his recuperation period. He never seemed quite the same again and left Worcestershire at the end of the 1938 season to join Rishton in the Lancashire League.

He returned to Australia and then went to South Africa where, in 1941-42, he played for Transvaal, so becoming one of the few players to have represented first-class sides, other than touring teams, in four different countries.

Where the importation of McDonald had caused an uproar because he was a mature cricketer of international standing, Warne, Jackson and Walsh were absorbed into the county scene. They were honest professionals earning an honest living, and the third place that Leicestershire reached in the championship in 1953 was the highest place that they or Worcestershire attained during the Warne–Walsh–Jackson period. The greatest hostility towards an overseas player in English cricket has always been shown towards the man whose presence has transformed the fortunes of a county, and, from the members of a county, towards players – such as Javed, Croft and Kapil Dev – who, having been paid large sums of money, failed to do so.

In the period between the wars, there was always an unease about players who were born abroad representing English counties, and this unease erupted into open conflict at international level in 1930.

In 1929 Duleepsinhji, who, although born in India, was educated at Cheltenham and Cambridge and played for Sussex from 1926 to 1932, was selected to play for England in the first Test against South Africa. After that first Test it was learned that the visitors objected to him representing England, for whom they did not recognise him as being qualified. On being made aware of this, Duleepsinhji, a young man of great charm, stood down for the rest of the series.

The following year the Australians raised no objection to Duleepsinhji playing in the England side, and he emulated his uncle, 'Ranji', in scoring a century in his first Test against the old enemy.

He was forced out of the game through ill health, and he had to decline an invitation to go to Australia with Jardine's side, 1932-33, his place being taken by the Nawab of Pataudi, who also hit a hundred in his first Test against Australia. Pataudi led the first Indian side to England after the Second World War, but, as he had represented England, special permission had to be granted by MCC to allow him to play for the country of his birth. Surprisingly, in November 1951, MCC approved his application to play again for Worcestershire, the county for whom he had played in the 1930s, stating that they regarded him as still qualified for the county, reasoning which some found hard to follow. His return to county cricket never came about, however, as he died a few weeks after his application had been granted. He was 41, and he had never enjoyed good health. His son was to play for Sussex and captain India.

The 1930 England–Australia series which witnessed the might of Bradman and the first appearance in these matches of Duleepsinhji, also saw the debut of G.O. Allen in Test cricket. That his selection was greeted in many quarters with a great deal of animosity will come as a surprise to most readers for whom he has become one of the grand old men of English cricket, his services to the game were recognised by a knighthood in 1986.

The selectors had come under fire for naming Duleepsinhji, but there was a precedent in that his uncle had played for England with distinction. The choice of Allen, however, was criticised because he had been born in Sydney, his uncle, R.C., had played for Australia, and he had not come to England until he was seven. In reporting on the Lord's Test, the occasion of Allen's debut, Trevor Wignell, in the *Daily Express*, was adamant that Allen should not be in the side.

'When it was first announced that he was among the thirteen, there was considerable adverse comment, but it was generally expected that the selectors would become acquainted with public opinion, and decide to omit him. The remarks when he was chosen in preference to English-born Sandham and Larwood were very scathing. It is a fact that if England wins with the aid of Allen a considerable amount of gilt will be off the gingerbread.'

In his biography of Allen, E.W. Swanton tends to dismiss this as gutter journalism or the stuff of the gossip columnist, but Wignell's view was endorsed by others. MCC were to use Allen's Australian connection to diplomatic advantage a few years later when they named him as captain for the peace-seeking tour of Australia in 1936-37. The wounds from the Bodyline tour remained unhealed, and although Allen had very little experience of captaincy, he was believed by those in authority to be the best choice. 'Moreover,' wrote Warner, 'his family connection with Australia was in his favour for an enterprise which was to be one of good-will.' In any case, Allen was in good company, for among other England captains not born in this country are Warner himself, Lord Harris, Jardine, Ted Dexter, Freddie Brown and Colin Cowdrey. One wonders what Trevor Wignell would have felt about an England side which included Allen Lamb and Chris Smith, but that point was still half a century distant.

PART 3
Before the Deluge

There was some exciting and entertaining cricket played during the years of the Second World War, and much of it had an international flavour about it. The British Empire XI toured the country playing charity matches and invariably included the West Indians, C.B. Clarke and E.B. Eytle, while service matches gave us the first sight of Keith Miller, Pepper and Pettiford from Australia, and Badcock and Rabone from New Zealand. Dempster played for the Army and James kept wicket for the RAF for whom, on one memorable occasion at Lord's, he took four catches off the bowling of Glamorgan's Austin Matthews to send back the first four Army batsmen.

James did not return to Northamptonshire after the war, and in 1946 Merritt could play only in mid-week matches because of league commitments. Dempster had moved to business in Birmingham and was expected to play for Warwickshire, but after three matches he left first-class cricket.

Jackson and Walsh belonged essentially to the post-war years of Leicestershire cricket, and their dual success was quickly apparent in 1946. Northants acquired the services of Carlos Bertram Clarke, the West Indian leg-break bowler, who had played three Tests in 1939. Clarke had qualified as a doctor and settled in England. He assisted Northants occasionally between 1946 and 1949 and then became the terror of club cricket in the London area. Amazingly, he reappeared in first-class cricket with Essex in 1959 and 1960, playing eighteen matches. He was then 41 years old.

The only overseas players to be appearing regularly as professionals in 1946 were Walsh and Jackson, and they were joined in 1947 by Laddie Outschoorn, from Ceylon, who played for

Worcestershire and by Tom Pritchard who had qualified for Warwickshire. Both men had played in the Birmingham League in 1946.

Outschoorn had played cricket in Singapore where he became a prisoner-of-war of the Japanese. He came to England when he was repatriated and played for Worcestershire for thirteen years, a good batsman and a brilliant close-to-the-wicket fielder. Tom Pritchard turned out to be the most significant overseas player to be recruited by a county since Lancashire signed Ted McDonald, although his arrival caused less fuss and no controversy.

Pritchard was born in New Zealand and played for Wellington from 1937 to 1941. He was a genuine fast bowler and a batsman capable of some ferocious hitting. He was very successful, and by 1940, he was New Zealand's leading bowler, destined, it was thought, to be the spearhead of their attack when Test cricket resumed. Twice, in junior matches, he took all ten wickets in an innings.

He joined the army and served in the Mediterranean sector where he met Tom Dollery, who was to become Warwickshire's first professional captain in 1949. Dollery was impressed with Pritchard as a bowler and as a man and persuaded him to come to England to play for Warwickshire. They were together in the Central Mediterranean Forces side which arrived in England in August 1945 and played at Lord's. Merritt was also in the team which included Test cricketers and future Test cricketers like Wellard, Emmett, McIntyre, Martin and Smailes.

A Lord's XI beat CMF by one wicket in a match played over two days, but Pritchard was most impressive. 'Fast and accurate, he helped his side to gain an unexpected lead by taking the last three wickets for four runs. He accomplished this good work despite wearing boots two inches too big – the best he could buy in the Middle East when chosen at short notice for the trip.'

Warwickshire were impressed and accepted Dollery's recommendation. Under the amended rules of qualification drawn up in June 1945, they applied to MCC for the special registration of Pritchard, but this was rejected, 'infuriatingly delayed', and the New Zealander could not take his place in the Warwickshire side until 1947.

In his first season, he took 93 wickets, missing several matches through strains and taking some time to acclimatise to the English conditions. He was overworked, but when he was fit and bowling flat out he was the fastest bowler in the country.

The following season, while England were wallowing against Australia, he took 172 wickets, a number beaten that year only by Jack Walsh. Against Yorkshire, at Edgbaston, he took four of the last five wickets for 18 runs in eight overs and brought Warwickshire their first victory over Yorkshire since 1893. He was selected to represent the Players at Lord's, and the *News Chronicle* named him as one of the five personalities of the year, dubbing him 'a great team man'.

In 1949 he took 113 inexpensive wickets and Warwickshire climbed to fourth in the table, a position they maintained the following season when Pritchard again passed a hundred wickets. Under the existing rules of qualification, he could not play for the New Zealanders when they toured England in 1949. In electing to play for Warwickshire, he had debarred himself from Test cricket.

By 1951 Pritchard had been joined in the Warwickshire side by another New Zealander, Ray Hitchcock, a hard-hitting batsman and useful leg-break and googly bowler. Hitchcock had played for Canterbury and worked his passage to England to seek a professional career with Warwickshire, whom he served with the utmost loyalty even beyond his playing days which ended in 1964.

Warwickshire entered the county championship in 1895 and won the title in 1911. Their second triumph came in 1950 when Tom Pritchard, in spite of a bad start to the season and an injury which prevented him from playing at the close, took 103 wickets in all matches.

In his first thirteen matches, he took only 38 wickets at 31.55 each; in his next four games, he took 36 wickets at 10.88. It would be wrong to ascribe the major part in Warwickshire's championship victory to Pritchard – Grove and Hollies had equal claims as bowlers and the *Birmingham Post* called them an 'extraordinary team of ordinary cricketers' 'superbly led' – but Pritchard, though his pace was to drop with the years, had given them a dimension which no other county in England possessed, although 1951 saw the advance of Statham and Trueman and the revival of England's hopes of finding a fast bowler.

The shoulder injury which hampered him at the end of the season restricted him in his benefit year, 1952, and he could not hold a regular place in the side, nor was he ever again a force with Warwickshire. He left them at the end of 1955 and played four games for Kent as an amateur in 1956, but the glory years had been those which had culminated in the title win of 1951.

Not everyone was happy with Warwickshire's championship victory, although none denied that at a time when dullness and mediocrity were paralysing the game, they played dynamic cricket, six of their matches being won inside two days. The concern that was expressed by non-supporters of the county was that only two of the side, Grove and Gardner, were born in Warwickshire. The attack had been anticipated by M.F.K. Fraser in an article in *Wisden* of 1950 entitled *Warwickshire's Ups and Downs*. He agreed that professional talent had come to Edgbaston from all over the world. They had used Test players Donnelly from New Zealand and Kardar from India, later Pakistan, as amateurs, and as well as Pritchard and Hitchcock, they were to engage as professionals in the decade after the war, Keith Dollery of Australia, Don Taylor from New Zealand, Derief Taylor from the West Indies and Ibadulla of Pakistan. They were also to sign a Swede, Christensen, but he did not play first-class cricket.

Fraser argued that Warwickshire were persistent challengers for the championship in 1949, and the president and committee were confident that it could be won in the near future. 'With a record membership and record support at their turnstiles, they are willing to back their confidence by outlay wherever it may be made usefully. There are critics of a policy which has turned the Warwickshire staff into a Cricket League of Nations; but the Birmingham public, nurtured on the liberal transfer system of soccer, will not worry where their cricket favourites come from so long as they play attractively and win matches.'

Fraser was thirty years ahead of his time with his sentiment, but the Warwickshire supporters backed his view. They had known Pritchard and Hitchcock only as Warwickshire players, and they did not stop to question that they were born some thousands of miles away. Both had become part of the community, and Hitch-cock was an outstanding rugby player with Nuneaton.

The Times, in fact, supported Fraser's view, congratulating Warwickshire on their title win and confounding the critics of their policy of importing Commonwealth players. The writer saw it as part of a long-term policy. 'Warwickshire have set out to provide the success which would gain support for the Club and at the same time quicken the playing interest of youth in the county so that some day soon, so they could hope, many young players from within their own borders will be fighting for places in the side. And beyond this plans have been laid for further improve-ment and expanding the accommodation of the Edgbaston ground, so that some time it may again be the scene of a Test match. Nothing succeeds like success and Warwickshire, after a long interval, have tested it once more.'

Test cricket was to return to Birmingham in 1957, but *Wisden* did not share the sanguine view of the Warwickshire policy as expressed in *The Times*. 'It would be a sorry day for cricket if players were bartered in the transfer market, but no one need fear such a happening for already the problem has been tackled and Warwickshire were one of the counties represented on the small committee which has tightened the special registration rules. Now only two new registrations are permitted each year by any county and from 1953 no county will be allowed more than ten specially registered players on their list including eight profes-sionals.'

Warwickshire were not to win the championship for another twenty-one years, and then with the help of four West Indian Test players, the product of another policy.

However deep the concern at Warwickshire's winning the title in 1951 with imported players, and however grave the feeling about the number of overseas players in county cricket, there seemed to be no slackening of the number of Commonwealth recruitments to English counties.

Kent had O'Linn and Leary from South Africa, and they were joined in 1954 by the Australian Pettiford. Northants had Austra-lians Livingston and Tribe, followed by Manning, another Australian, in 1955. Nottinghamshire were well served by the

Australian all-rounder Bruce Dooland and the Sri Lankan Goonesena, who was an amateur, and they had the services of another Australian, Walker. Lancashire had Grieves from Australia, and Sussex had the South African, Foreman; both were soccer players. Warwickshire added Shirley Griffiths to their overseas contingent for a couple of seasons at the end of the fifties. He was a West Indian fast bowler who never quite fulfilled his potential.

For two seasons, Leicestershire had the help of Sargent as well as Jackson and Walsh, and McMahon, after six seasons with Surrey, moved to Somerset where he joined a strong overseas group, including, at one time or another, McCool, Wight, Yawar Saaed and Bill Alley. Since 1946, the number of overseas players had increased ten-fold.

For nine seasons, however, from 1952 to 1960, the championship was dominated by two counties who included only English-born players, Surrey and Yorkshire. McMahon, the Australian, who had joined Surrey in 1947, played seventeen matches in 1952 and 1953 and then joined Somerset on special registration for the 1954 season. That there were Commonwealth cricketers of high quality representing English counties in the 1950s is undeniable; but that there were none whose presence and ability could change a moderate side into one capable of challenging the supremacy of the great Surrey is equally true.

Most counties accepted their fate. Of the seventeen first-class counties, only ten had ever won the championship between 1864 and 1960, and of those ten, Glamorgan and Derbyshire had only won it once. There was only one honour for which to contend each year, and invariably that went to Yorkshire or Surrey. Followers of the other counties were content to enjoy good cricket and good players. It was not customary to worry too much about the result. Yet, having said that, the seven outstanding Commonwealth players in county cricket in the 1950s, six Australians and a West Indian, all made significant contributions and raised their sides to a level which, in three cases, had never before been attained. In 1957, Northamptonshire recorded fifteen championship victories, a county record, and finished second to Surrey, although 94 points adrift. The backbone of the side was the batting of Brookes, the captain, and Livingston, and the

57

bowling of Tyson, Tribe and Manning.

'Jock' Livingston, troubled by a knee injury, was in his last season with Northants, whom he had joined in 1950 after playing in the Lancashire League and captaining a Commonwealth side on a successful tour of India. A hard-hitting left-handed batsman and occasional wicket-keeper, Livingston played for New South Wales before coming to England.

For South Australia, where he returned after his spell with Northants, John Manning took 66 wickets between 1951 and 1954. He was a slow left-arm bowler and a useful batsman. He was qualified for Northants by 1955, took 116 wickets in 1956 and 104 in 1957, when he was one of the players responsible for Northants finishing runners-up in the county championship. He was forced out of the game through injury in 1960.

The career of George Tribe in many ways mirrors that of Albert Trott, for it was his omission from the Australian party that came to England in 1948 that caused him to forsake his own country. He was one of the greatest of unorthodox left-arm spinners and he developed into a batsman consistently capable of a thousand runs a season. For Northants, he did the 'double' seven times.

The war interrupted his cricket career, and he did not make his first-class debut for Victoria until 1945-46. The following season he helped the state to win the Sheffield Shield, taking 33 wickets at 17.54 each. He was by far and away the outstanding bowler of the season and played in the first two Tests against England, but with little success. He was also selected for the fifth Test, but he failed to take a wicket and he was not named in the side to come to England. It was a short-sighted decision because he revelled in conditions in this country, but the Australian side of 1948 had an abundance of talent. Tribe was already 28 when that side toured, so it was obvious that his chances of forcing his way into the Australian side again were limited. Anxious to earn his living as a cricketer, he signed for Milnrow in the Central Lancashire League.

His success was phenomenal. He followed his 136 wickets in his first season with 148 in 1948 and a record 150 in 1949. He then moved to Rawtenstall in the Lancashire League. He was approached by Lancashire, but declined the opportunity to play county cricket because of his league commitments.

He was an engineer by profession, a fact which had caused him to be brought out of the army during the war to work in a reserved occupation, and he followed this work in England in the close season. In 1952 he was engaged by a Northampton firm, and he joined the county side. In his first four matches for them, he took 40 wickets, and he maintained his standard of excellence until he retired in 1959, completing the 'double' in his last season when he was 39.

The reasons for George Tribe leaving Australia and seeking a cricket career in England were similar to those that prompted Colin McCool and Bill Alley to do the same. McCool was the star of the first Australia–England Test series after the war, taking eighteen wickets with his leg-breaks and hitting 272 runs, average 54, in the five matches. He was troubled by a sore spinning finger on the tour of England, 1948, and did not play in a Test, and before the 1953 tour of England, he went into league cricket with the East Lancashire club. In 1956, aged forty, he joined Somerset, for whom he played for five seasons with distinction.

Bill Alley did not play for Somerset until he was 38, and was 51 when he retired. Alley had been near to selection for the Australian side to New Zealand in 1946, and he was bitterly disappointed when he was not included in the party. A very hard-hitting left-handed batsman and a medium-pace bowler, he played excitingly for New South Wales. The Australian selectors, he believed, thought him too old to begin a Test career at the age of 29, so he accepted an offer to join Colne in the Lancashire League. He had rejected a contract with Rawtenstall, but recommended a young friend, Ken Grieves, to the club, and Grieves later played for Lancashire.

Alley emphasised, 'The exodus of young Australian cricketers after the war – more than half a potential Test team left to try their luck in England in the late 1940s and early 1950s – was a bombshell for the Australian administrators.' Certainly the losses were not felt by Australia immediately, but by the mid-fifties they were beginning to suffer from the defections of the past decade.

Keith Miller and Bob Cristofani were approached by Rawtenstall, and Cecil Pepper, a tremendous entertainer and a potential Test cricketer, sacrificed a first-class career to play league cricket where he was an immense favourite. Mankad, the great Indian all-rounder, also entertained the Lancashire League and although it restricted his appearances for India, he was able to continue with a long and very successful international career. Australia were less accommodating to their league professionals. According to Alley, league players were not even welcome at state level. 'There was no question, either, of us playing for New South Wales. The bitterness was so deep that the State selectors wouldn't entertain the idea of us as guest players.'

Alley prospered in the Lancashire League. Following the trail that Constantine had blazed in the thirties, it was studded with players of high quality – Hazare, Weekes, Dooland, Freer, Lindwall – and Alley was a dynamic and popular entertainer.

In 1953 he moved to Blackpool and played for them for four years, hitting twenty centuries in the Northern League. He looked for a long-term contract from Blackpool, for whom he was averaging over a hundred, but it was not forthcoming, and, at the age of 39, he was specially registered for Somerset.

Lancashire had been the first to approach Alley, on the instigation of Ken Grieves, but some considered that he was too old and that he would need to change his aggressive style if he were to survive in county cricket. Tom Goddard motivated an offer from Gloucestershire, but the money could not match what he was earning in salary and collections at Colne. Nottinghamshire made a lucrative offer, but they were insistent that he would bat low in the order and have to keep wicket. Kent also approached him, but it was Somerset who persevered and got their man. They offered him an initial contract of three years and a benefit after five seasons.

There was no opposition as to his immediate registration because of his age. The MCC could not have realised that he was to play for Somerset until 1968, and then he only retired because they offered him a contract for one-day matches rather than a full contract. He hit over 18,000 runs for them and took more than 700 wickets, did the 'double' in 1962 and took 62 wickets in 1961, the year he hit an incredible 3,019 runs.

Somerset had finished bottom of the county championship for four successive seasons, from 1952 to 1955, and in 1956 they were fifteenth. In Alley's first season, they jumped to eighth, and the following season, with both him and McCool playing a decisive role, they finished third, the highest position that they had attained since 1892, when the championship consisted of only twelve counties. It is a position that has not been bettered since.

The strength of Alley's contribution to Somerset cricket, and more briefly McCool's, was that he had total commitment to it. He bought a smallholding near Taunton, enjoyed the local scrumpy cider and met the locals at skittles. They never looked on him as a passing stranger. He was as much a Somerset man as if he had spent all his life amid the Quantocks.

What was also important about Alley and Somerset was the help and encouragement that he gave to young players on the staff. That is a service and a quality which is immeasurable and cannot be determined by reference to the score-book.

It is hard to look upon Bill Alley as an overseas player. It was in England, in Lancashire and Somerset, that he became a legend, noted for his cricket and his repartee. He never played for Australia, but he was a better player than many who did, particularly at the time when he was the idol of Somerset.

Alley's first season at Somerset coincided with Bruce Dooland's last year at Nottinghamshire, where he had spent five years. Dooland was the most successful leg-break bowler in county cricket since the days of 'Tich' Freeman, and his 368 wickets in his first two seasons, 1953 and 1954, emulated the great man. He was also a competent batsman and twice reached a thousand runs in a season, so completing the 'double'.

Dooland performed the first 'hat-trick' in Australian first-class cricket after the war, for South Australia against Victoria, and won a place on the trip to New Zealand. He was selected for the third and fourth Tests against Hammond's side and did reasonably well, but he and Tribe seemed to be contending for the same place, and the left-arm bowler was brought back for the last Test. The following season, 1947-48, Dooland played in one Test against India, but he was given little opportunity and was not selected in the party to come to England, Ring being preferred.

Like Alley and Tribe, Dooland felt thwarted and signed for East Lancashire, for whom he played for four years with great success, the club winning two trophies in his time with them. Nottinghamshire invited him to join them and, having qualified by residence, he made his debut for them against Kent at Trent Bridge.

Notts had not been higher than eleventh in the championship table since the end of the war, and for the past three seasons they had been in the bottom three. 'Dooland, more than anyone, transformed the Nottinghamshire side,' *Wisden* reported. 'As often happens with cricketers of his calibre, Dooland's bowling made that of his partners more effective.'

The county finished eighth in 1953 and fifth in 1954. After Dooland's return to Australia they slipped back into the bottom three for ten of the next eleven seasons. They adopted a youth policy which failed to produce quite the quality that they had hoped for, and their leading bowler for most of the sixties was a West Indian, Carlton Forbes.

Notts sank so low in morale and support that Keith Miller, newly elected as a member of MCC and anxious to play for the club, appeared for the county as a guest in the match against Cambridge University at Trent Bridge in 1959. He hit 62 and 102 not out, took two wickets, and the next week, playing for MCC against Oxford University, pulled a calf muscle and ended his career.

Until the mid-sixties Ted McDonald remained the one star player to have been imported by a county with a view to bringing honours to that county. Pritchard, Dooland, McCool, Tribe, Alley, Livingston and Manning all did much to revive the fortunes of their counties, and Pritchard contributed significantly towards Warwickshire's title win, but none of them was an established star when he came to this country. McCool, with fourteen Test matches to his credit, was by far the most experienced international, but his achievements for Australia were well in the past by the time he joined Somerset.

The overseas players in county cricket in the fifties were almost exclusively Australians who had come to county cricket via the leagues, yet from that point on, as emphases in the game changed and Test cricket proliferated, the Australians were to be very much in the minority.

The West Indians had made a tremendous impact on English cricket with their victories in the Test matches of 1950, and several of that famous side, Worrell, Weekes and Ramadhin, had gone into the northern leagues, but none had been tempted into county cricket until Roy Marshall joined Hampshire in 1954.

Marshall was the youngest player in the West Indian party in 1950, scored over a thousand runs, but did not play in a Test. He played two Test matches against Australia, and two against New Zealand, in 1951-52, but his engagement by Hampshire brought an end to his Test career. A gloriously free batsman and an occasional off-break bowler, he was approached by Lowerhouse at the end of the 1950 tour and signed to play for them in the Lancashire League.

He was only 21 when he first played in the League and he did not enjoy great success. On the 1950 tour, he had scored an exciting century against Hampshire, but he was surprised when, in 1952, he received a letter from Desmond Eagar inviting him to play for Hampshire. He hesitated to accept because he still nursed dreams of establishing a place in the West Indian side. He played for Barbados and was named as twelfth man for the second Test against India, in 1952-53, but he realised that he would not disturb Rae and Stollmeyer as the West Indies opening pair and he signed the contract that Hampshire had offered him. Later, when he had become one of the most exciting players to be seen in county cricket, he would say that batting with Frank Worrell at the other end had brought him a realisation of his own limitations.

From the day that Marshall signed for them, Hampshire have never been without a West Indian on their staff.

In his autobiography, Marshall offered several reasons for turning his back on Test cricket and joining Hampshire. His eagerness to play cricket six days a week was the decisive factor. 'In those days the West Indies didn't have such a full fixture list as they have nowadays. First-class cricket itself was very limited because there was no Shell tournament as they have between the islands today. I knew no other life than cricket and I was hungry to play it at the highest standard I could find, as often as I could.'

Money was a minor consideration. Hampshire offered him £800 a year, and if they found him a job, the wages would be deducted from that.

His first match for Hampshire was in 1953 while he was fulfilling his residential qualification. He played against the Australians at Southampton at the beginning of June, took four for 69 with his off-breaks to bring about a collapse and then hit a thrilling 71 in 95 minutes, with five sixes. It was an appetiser for the Hampshire supporters and gave them some indication of what he was to provide over the next fifteen years.

He had arrived in Southampton on 21 April 1953, and began his residential qualification from that date. In 1955 he was set to take his place in the county side. His impact was immediate. A side that had never been above fifth in the county championship, and that 41 years previously, and that had not finished in the top half of the table since the war, ended the 1955 season in third place. Marshall topped both the batting and the bowling averages, and record crowds were attracted to Hampshire grounds.

'What was the reason for this sudden advance of Hampshire cricket?' asked the skipper Desmond Eagar, and answered the question himself. 'Undoubtedly Roy Marshall had much to do with it. Not because he made nearly 1,900 runs, nor even that he made them so attractively, but because by his method he gave confidence to the rest of the side and showed them by his example that the ball was there to be hit. Marshall did a great service to Hampshire cricket.'

It was only a taster of the joys that were to come. 'It is hardly possible,' wrote Eagar in another context, 'to overestimate his contribution to county cricket and to Hampshire in particular. His batting was one of the most thrilling experiences of the 1950s and 1960s. Had he been born an Englishman he must have been an automatic Test selection. His policy was to dictate to the bowler before the bowler could dictate to him. That was why he liked to open the innings. Occasionally his aggression brought about his downfall, but more often spectators were able to glory in the power of his cutting, in his driving through the covers and in his magnificent hitting wide of mid-on.'

At first he was conscious that the county game was harder than

The first 'cricket mercenary', the Australian Billy Midwinter, with his Gloucestershire team-mates in 1877. When the Australian tourists borrowed him the following year, W.G. snatched him back.

F.R. Spofforth, the 'demon' of Australia, Derbyshire, Wembley Park and Hampstead.

Albert Trott, turn of the century hitter with a liking for the Lord's pavilion.

K.S. Ranjitsinhji in 1895, the year he joined Sussex. The following year he scored a brilliant century on his Test debut for England against Australia.

The Nawab of Pataudi, another Indian prince who made a hundred in his first Test for England. He also hit a double century for Oxford in the Varsity match, and later captained India.

His son and successor as Nawab, who in 1961 scored two centuries in the same match for Oxford against the champion county, Yorkshire, before joining Sussex. He too went on to captain India.

The fearsome E.A. McDonald, in Pelham Warner's words 'the best fast bowler that Australia has ever sent us'. After a spell with the Nelson club he joined Lancashire in 1924.

Learie Constantine, the dynamic West Indian who played for Nelson in the 1930s. His all-round talent revitalised club and League, but his colour was unacceptable to Lancashire.

Roy Marshall, a gloriously free batsman who joined Hampshire in 1953, since when there has always been a West Indian on the staff.

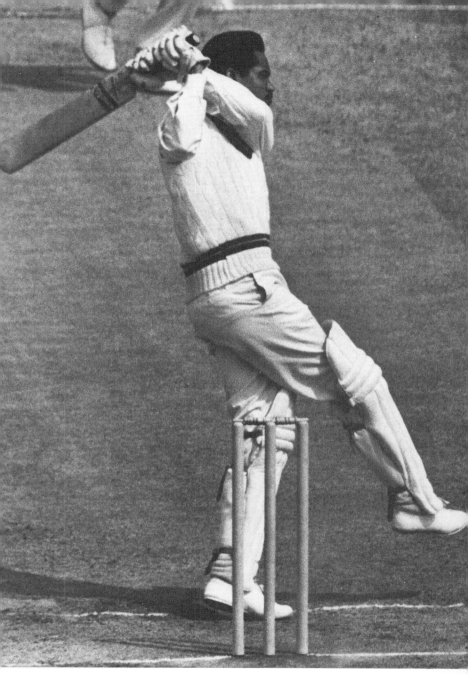

Gary Sobers, the undisputed king of cricket in the late sixties. Notts were quick to sign him when the immediate registration rule came into being in 1968, and made him captain, but the hard work of continuous cricket became less attractive to him as the years passed.

Barry Richards, arguably the finest batsman since Bradman, who signed for Hampshire in 1968. For nearly a decade he and Gordon Greenidge formed a devastating opening pair. Behind the stumps is Farokh Engineer of India and Lancashire.

Mike Procter, Gloucestershire's superb
South African all-rounder. 'In full cry,
he was a wonderful sight, a magnificent
blend of invincible power and human
vulnerability.'

Back in 1965 it looked as if both Procter and Richards might play for Gloucestershire. Instead their competitive encounters gave an added spice to Hants–Glos matches.

he expected. He realised that for the average player, victory and a high place in the championship could mean bonus money and a better standard of living. He was also aware that personal success could bring a Test place and an even higher income. He quickly adapted to this, sensitive always to the needs and ambitions of his colleagues and opponents.

In 1958, with Ingleby-Mackenzie now leading the side, Hampshire surpassed their efforts of three years earlier and finished second in the championship. The title had seemed within their grasp until the closing weeks of the season when they collapsed, allowing Surrey to move ahead of them and win the championship for the seventh successive year. Marshall scored over two thousand runs in all matches and was chosen as one of *Wisden*'s Five Cricketers of the Year. In carrying the Hampshire batting on his shoulders, along with his opening partner Gray, he was not constricted in his approach to the game, still playing with a freedom that delighted all who watched him. He appeared for the Players against the Gentlemen at Lord's, and although he had to retire for a while with a cut chin, he scored briskly and played one cover drive of such exquisite beauty and power as to reverberate down the memory of nearly thirty years.

In 1960 Hampshire added another West Indian to their staff when they obtained a special registration for Danny Livingstone. Born in Antigua, he came to Hampshire via Canada and the Birmingham League. He played against Oxford University in 1959 and was contracted and registered in time for the following season. He was a hard-hitting left-handed batsman who provided the Hampshire middle order with a strength that it had been lacking.

By now, Marshall had virtually ceased to bowl, but his strength in batting was as consistent as ever. In 1961 Hampshire took the title for the first time in their history, and he passed two thousand runs for the third year in succession.

The title was won when Derbyshire were beaten at Bournemouth on the first day of September even though Derbyshire's West Indian, Johnson, gave the Hampshire bowling something of a thrashing. As ever, Marshall played a significant part in that victory, and Norman Preston's notes in *Wisden* selected him, 'one of the few enterprising opening batsmen in the country', for special mention. 'He is now qualified for England and he could go to Australia. That Hampshire won the Championship for the first time in their history was due largely to his virulent and exciting attitude to each and every bowler he faced.'

Preston continued with praise of Marshall's courage, authority and eagerness to take on bowlers of the calibre of Statham and Trueman. His point on Marshall's eligibility for England is an interesting one, and the cause of some confusion both to the editor of *Wisden* and to the chairman of selectors, Walter Robins.

According to Marshall, when he was playing for MCC against Surrey at Lord's, at the beginning of May 1962, he was approached by Robins who asked him if he was interested in playing Test cricket. After some moments of trepidation Marshall realised what a magnificent opportunity was being presented to him and sought Robins out in the tea interval to say that he would be delighted. Before he could give his answer, however, Robins informed him that he had made enquiries and found that Marshall was not eligible for England. The MCC Advisory Committee had ruled that anybody who had played for one country could not be chosen for England. This was in contradiction to the rules of the Imperial Cricket Conference which stated:

'A cricketer unless debarred by the Imperial Cricket Conference shall be entitled to play for any country in which he is residing and has been residing during the four immediately preceding years provided that he has not played for the country of his birth during that period.'

Marshall had not played for West Indies for ten years.

In 1957, before the West Indies selected their side to tour England, he was contacted by the West Indies Board of Control who asked him if he would like to be considered for the tour. Reluctantly, he had to decline the invitation. Under the existing qualification law, it would have meant breaking his contract to play for West Indies in 1957, and he would have had to spend another two years qualifying before becoming eligible for championship cricket again.

Five years later, he received an unofficial approach from Frank Worrell who wanted him as Conrad Hunte's opening partner for the 1963 tour, but for the same reasons he once again declined. Not surprisingly, he is rather envious of West Indian and other cricketers who play county cricket today and are still able to enjoy a full Test career.

Marshall captained Hampshire from 1966 to 1970 and ended his career in 1972. Ironically, Hampshire were to win the title the following year, but much in the game had changed by then.

Brian Hayward, in *Wisden*, expressed the sadness that all felt in seeing Marshall leave first-class cricket, saying that for nearly twenty years Marshall had been the greatest entertainer in county cricket. In his last season, at the age of 42, he was still a batsman of the highest calibre and played a magnificent innings of 203 against Derbyshire. 'To say that he will be missed is a gross understatement.'

When Marshall entered county cricket he was one of sixteen overseas players in the first-class game in England; by the time he left it, the number was close on seventy.

Following Hampshire's championship win in 1961, Yorkshire won the title five times in seven years, since when no county has been triumphant without the aid of an overseas player.

When Worcestershire broke the Yorkshire sequence in 1964 and 1965 they owed much to opening batsman Ron Headley, the son of George Headley, the greatest of West Indian batsmen in the years before the war. Ron Headley, a left-handed batsman and brilliant fielder, first played in 1958 at the age of nineteen, but did not command a regular place in the side, after he had qualified, until 1961. He played county cricket before he played domestic cricket for Jamaica, in 1965-66, and was luckier than Marshall, for the regulations were changed so that he was able to represent the West Indies in two Tests in 1973.

Leicestershire had the assistance of two fine batsmen from Sri Lanka in the 1960s, Inman and Jayasinghe. Both sought to follow a professional career in England because the opportunities for first-class cricket in their own country at the time were almost non-existent.

In 1964 and 1965 Lancashire engaged Sonny Ramadhin. He had tormented England in 1950, becoming immortalised in West Indian cricket history when, with his colleague Valentine, he had spun his side to victory in the Test at Lord's. He remembers cricket that year as 'fun', 'because all the players played the game as it should be played'.

Seven years later, at Edgbaston, Ramadhin took seven for 49 in the first innings, but, in the second, May and Colin Cowdrey added 411 for the fourth wicket and effectively ended the dominance that Ramadhin had had over English batsmen. The little spinner played Test cricket for four more years and then settled in England. He still runs a public house near Oldham. Cowdrey, in particular, thwarted him with pad play. 'He played with his bat behind his pads and he just kept padding me away so that I couldn't get through. I kept appealing for l.b.w. and, as the laws are today, he could have been out, but not then. He could use his pads outside the off stump without playing a shot.'

In 1964, when his Test career was over and his place in the West Indian side had been taken by Lance Gibbs, Ramadhin signed a five-year contract with Lancashire, but he played for only two seasons. 'I found it very hard in county cricket. I was all right in the morning and until tea-time, but the last two hours were very hard and I left after a couple of seasons. Cricket had changed. There was a more professional approach. It was never quite the same for spinners after that.'

Cricket had indeed changed and by the end of the 1950s grave concern was being expressed as to its future. In 1961, when there was joy at Hampshire winning the championship with a positive approach to the game, there was also a sense of malaise in the game. There seemed to be a total lack of enterprise and imagination. The county captains had met at Lord's some six weeks before the season opened and 'expressed their unanimous determination to provide entertaining cricket during the coming season'. They were to 'encourage a more aggressive approach in batting'. However good their intentions, there was little sign of a change in attitudes among the counties in the way in which games were conducted. As late as 1967, when points in the county championship were only awarded for a win and for a first innings lead, Hampshire and Middlesex met at Lord's on the first three days of July and could not produce a first innings result over the three days. Only twelve minutes' play were lost over the three days, and Marshall began the match with an innings of 153 in three hours, but the rest of the match was tedium and stalemate.

It was a situation which called for desperate measures, but by this time radical changes in the structure of the game had already been implemented.

Seven years earlier, in 1960, the Advisory County Cricket Committee had asked MCC to set up a committee of inquiry to examine the problems confronting the game. These problems came under three main headings: finance, structure and conduct or attitude.

Their interim report, while still clinging to traditional values, suggested a change in structure which would allow for the introduction of a *one-day* knock-out competition.

This competition, originally sponsored by Gillette, came into operation in 1963, the year which also marked the end of the demarcation between amateurs and professionals. The last match between the Gentlemen and the Players was played in 1962, and from then on, all were known as *cricketers.*

Although the sixty-over knock-out competition had been greeted with much apprehension in some quarters, its success was immediate. Very large crowds watched the matches, especially the later rounds, and the final itself, between Sussex and Worcestershire, drew a capacity crowd to Lord's. Instant cricket had proved a financial success although, on the tactical side, the game had shown two disturbing tendencies. One was that the majority of counties were reluctant to include even one slow bowler in their side; the other was that field-placings, including Dexter's in the final, saw seven or eight men spread around the boundary.

There was concern, too, that the atmosphere at the final was more like what one would find at a soccer match than what one usually associated with cricket, and the crowd came on to the pitch at the end of the game.

The movement which had brought about the abolition of the distinction between amateur and professional and the introduction of limited-over cricket rolled on to bring changes in the administrative structure of the game. In 1965, the Imperial Cricket Conference became the International Cricket Conference and introduced associate membership which was to incorporate countries like Denmark, Holland and Argentina, which were cricket-playing, but not of Test-match status. Three years later, the Test and County Cricket Board, the corporate voice of the counties, effectively became the governing body of the game, deciding matters which were once the concern of the Advisory County Cricket Committee and the Board of Control, both of which were arms of the MCC.

More significant, though as yet only dimly perceived, was that the evolutionary process which had wrought these changes was also bringing a change in the attitudes of those who watched the game. For more than a hundred years people were content to watch a day's cricket, delighting in the skills of batsman and bowler and in the intrinsic beauty of the game itself. The championship was dominated by a handful of strong counties, and the remainder were content with their brief moments of glory like a victory over Yorkshire or the establishing of a club record. The joy of watching a day's cricket was mostly unhampered by concern as to who, ultimately, won or lost.

By the 1960s, this attitude was dying for all but the purists. We had moved into the age of success, when a man became judged by the extent of his material possessions. In cricket it meant that many were no longer concerned for the game itself; they demanded that the side they followed should be successful. Suddenly there was pressure on committees and players to win something. If they did not, or at least were not challenging for honours, their support would melt away.

It was this search for success, demanded by supporters, and vital to county finances, which was to bring about a radical change in the rules that governed the importation and registration of overseas players.

PART 4
The Flood-gates Open

In 1963, the first important changes in the rules governing the registration of overseas players came about. If a cricketer born overseas had resided in England for five consecutive years, the residential period of qualification for a county was reduced to one year. In other circumstances, it remained at two. More pointedly, during the English off-season a registered player was no longer debarred from playing first-class cricket overseas as long as he had the permission of his county. An overseas cricketer was, however, still debarred from playing for the country of his birth on a tour of England. It was still stipulated that no county should have more than two cricketers born overseas on their list of registered players in any one season.

In the mid-sixties, however, the registration of an overseas player still necessitated a period of qualification which some found frustrating. Basil D'Oliveira came to England in 1960, unable, by dint of his colour, to follow a first-class career in his native South Africa. He was given a trial contract by the Central Lancashire League side Middleton and served them splendidly for three years. His gratitude to Middleton is undying. 'They picked me up from nothing and turned me into a county player.' Worcestershire invited him to join them but he first had to fulfil the necessary residential qualification even though no one was contesting Worcestershire's right to play him. The player himself, then aged 33, found it irksome.

'Before I could play championship cricket for Worcester, I had to complete a year's qualifying period. It meant a return to League cricket – this time with Kidderminster in the Birmingham League – and the occasional non-championship appearance in the county side.

'I can't say that I accepted it graciously. The year 1964 irked me. Having reached this stage in my cricket development I had no patience with the delay. I wanted first-class cricket. At my age, when the number of seasons in front of me must be limited, I could not afford even a year.'

So D'Oliveira could not play championship cricket for Worcestershire until 1965, but a year later, having been resident in England for more than five years and not being required by the country of his birth, he was in the England Test team.

The relaxation of the restriction preventing an overseas cricketer representing his country was a significant advance. Mushtaq Mohammad, the youngest Test debutant, signed a five-year contract for Northamptonshire in 1964 and was qualified for the county championship by 1966. When Pakistan toured England in 1967 Mushtaq played for them in the three Tests and in one other first-class match while assisting Northants for the rest of the season. It is worth noting *Wisden*'s comment in relation to Mushtaq and others.

'The invitations to four Pakistan-based cricketers from England, Mushtaq, Intikhab, Ibadulla and Nasim-ul-Ghani, although viewed with disfavour in certain quarters, could not have been wholly condemned. The policy was partially successful. Having seen these cricketers in action from their early days, I found that since they had turned professional, their very approach to the game had undergone a perceptible change. That attitude smacked of safety-first. From gay cavaliers they had become plodders, eschewing all kinds of risk.'

Another viewpoint might emphasise that experience in English league and county cricket had transformed embryo internationals into hardened Test players.

There was now an increasing number of people who supported the idea that more overseas players should be encouraged into county cricket. Barry Richards and Mike Procter, the South Africans, appeared for Gloucestershire against the South African touring side of 1965, but, according to *Playfair Cricket Annual*, 'they have returned to South Africa and will not play again for the county'.

Essex and Kent brought two unknown players from Barbados,

Keith Boyce and John Shepherd, and, having served their two-year period of residential qualification, they gave outstanding service to their respective counties.

The registration committee still kept a most watchful eye on proceedings. On 20 April 1966 Cheshire applied for the special registration of Ken Grieves who had left Lancashire in 1964, but Lancashire refused to sign the agreement form allowing Grieves to play for Cheshire because he had broken his contract in putting his name to a series of articles detrimental to cricket within twenty-four months of playing for the county. Cheshire appealed against this ruling two months later, but Lancashire's objection was upheld.

On 4 May 1966 it was reported that Basharat Hassan for Notts and Tony Greig for Sussex had begun their twenty-four months residential qualifying period. At the beginning of 1967, however, Greig appealed against the imposition of the two-year period under the amendment to rule 5(d) which allowed a cricketer in his circumstances to serve only a one-year period of qualification. The appeal was upheld, and Greig made his county championship debut against Lancashire a few months later when he scored a magnificent 156.

The Greig saga did not end with his qualification for Sussex in 1967. In April 1968 the committee on registration were asked to reconsider Greig's status and to approve the Sussex claim that he be recognised as English-born. The evidence to support Greig was that his father had a family business in the United Kingdom which he visited at regular intervals, and he himself now held a British passport and was permanently resident in the United Kingdom. The committee rejected the appeal, however, agreeing unanimously that the player, who had been born in South Africa, could not be considered an English-born cricketer until he had resided permanently in the country for five years as required by rule 7(d).

In October 1973 the committee was again asked to reconsider Greig's position, but again they ruled that under the existing regulations Greig was an overseas player. By that time, he had already played for England in nineteen Test matches.

Another long running saga began in 1965 when Younis Ahmed

played one game for Surrey, against the South African tourists. He did not play in 1966, but he was qualified to appear in the county championship in 1967. He was only seventeen when he first played for Surrey although he had had some first-class experience in Pakistan, to which he returned after he had completed his residential qualification. In October 1969 it was ruled that as he had resided in England for five years, he could play in Pakistan without jeopardising his qualification for Surrey. A few weeks later, he played in two Test matches for Pakistan against New Zealand.

In 1972-73, he played for South Australia in the Sheffield Shield. This was not a good move. Pollard reports, 'He was an unsatisfactory import with the South Australian players, most of whom believed his place should have gone to a young local batsman rather than a player with an unremarkable past overseas. This feeling was partly caused by reports that Younis was to receive $1-a-run while playing for South Australia.'

In October 1976 it was stated that although he had played for Pakistan in 1969, Younis now wished to be recognised as qualifying for England. The necessary period of qualification was ten years after his last Test appearance for Pakistan, but the committee could use their discretionary powers and reduce the period to eight years. The decision was important to Surrey, who had Geoff Howarth and Intikhab Alam as registered overseas players and were anxious to add a fast bowler to their staff, but the county were thwarted when Pakistan objected to Younis being recognised as English.

The argument on behalf of Younis was that his means of earning a livelihood was threatened. In December 1977 the committee regretted that it was still impossible to accede to Surrey's request to have Younis recognised as English, but they would reconsider the matter after the 1968 season if Younis's career was in jeopardy. Surrey did not re-engage Younis after the 1968 season, and they obtained the services of Sylvester Clarke. In order to make it possible for Younis to continue earning a living by playing cricket, the TCCB sub-committee on registration recognised him as English, under their discretionary powers, and he signed for Worcestershire.

He played for Worcestershire until 1983 when he left in mid-season after it was disclosed that he had bet against his side. He joined Glamorgan in 1984 but left towards the end of the 1986 season, again in less than happy circumstances, to concentrate on his business career.

Three other notable cricketers went through the process of residential qualification in the mid-sixties, the West Indian Lance Gibbs for Warwickshire, the New Zealander Glenn Turner for Worcestershire, and the South African Hylton Ackerman for Northamptonshire. All three began their period of residence in April 1967 and played for their counties in non-championship matches that season. At the end of the season, Northants applied that Ackerman should be granted permission to take a holiday in South Africa during the winter. The holiday was authorised on the same terms that had been granted to Tony Greig, that he was allowed a holiday of *two months door to door*, provided he played no first-class cricket while in South Africa. In February 1968 it was reported that Ackerman had broken his residential qualification by remaining in South Africa for more than eight weeks. Nevertheless, he appeared in championship matches that year and assisted Northants until 1971.

Glenn Turner was unquestionably one of the most successful of overseas players ever to appear in county cricket, and arguably, in spite of his 41 Test matches for New Zealand, a product of English cricket – in that of his 455 first-class games, 284 were for Worcestershire and only 130 for New Zealand sides outside Tests. On top of that, he played in numerous John Player League, Benson and Hedges Cup and Gillette Cup matches for the midland county.

He had become obsessed by the game at school and came under the influence of Billy Ibadulla, the Pakistani cricketer who played for Warwickshire and coached in New Zealand. Ibadulla suggested that he could succeed in county cricket and arranged for him to have a trial with Warwickshire. Turner worked on the night shift at a bakery in Dunedin for a year in order to raise the fare to England, but shortly before he was due to leave he received a telephone call from Mike Smith, the Warwickshire captain, saying that one of the committee had almost certainly signed an overseas player (at that time Warwickshire had both Gibbs and Owen Williams about to start qualifying) and that the county would, in consequence, have a full quota of overseas players. Warwickshire would, however, still honour the two-month trial contract that they had offered Turner.

The young man was in a quandary, but decided to come to England as planned. He found Smith and Warwickshire most helpful as they provided him with money for kit and arranged trials with other counties. Worcestershire was the nearest county with whom a trial had been arranged so he went there first. He spent two days in the nets watched by Tom Graveney and Don Kenyon, and he was offered a contract worth £650.

In 1967 he played mainly second eleven cricket while appearing for Stourbridge in the Birmingham League on Saturdays. He was qualified for the championship in 1968, having spent the winter of 1967-68 in England to meet the demands of the residential qualification. It was the only winter he was to spend in England. He scored 1,182 runs in 1968, but he became known as 'the strokeless wonder' on the county circuit. Five years later, he was to reach a thousand runs by the end of May, and he was to become one of the most reliable and aggressive batsmen in limited-over cricket.

Worcestershire's opening batsmen at the beginning of the 1968 season were Duncan Fearnley and the West Indian Ron Headley. Turner batted in the middle order, but later moved up to open, Fearnley dropping down to number four or five. With Turner having proved himself, Fearnley was not re-engaged at the end of the season. After seven seasons with the county in which he had not been capped Duncan Fearnley had become one of the first young English professionals whose career had been blighted because of the importation of an overseas cricketer. Fearnley, now chairman of Worcestershire, bears no malice. He and Turner have remained firm friends and business acquaintances, and Fearnley has thrived with his cricket equipment organisation, but, undeniably, the arrival of Turner cost Fearnley a career in first-class cricket.

Within six months of the end of his first full season in England, Turner was in the New Zealand side. Two years earlier, he had left his home country at the age of nineteen, raw and untried.

It is interesting to note Turner's comments on his reaction to domestic cricket in New Zealand once he had established himself at Worcestershire. 'I tended to come back to New Zealand wanting more than anything to relax, to do nothing more than simply walk along a deserted beach. While it was nice to make a few runs at home now and then I found it hard to work up the enthusiasm to go out and produce my best throughout the New Zealand season as well as the English one. I always felt as if I was on trial when playing at home, that other players were measuring their ability against me, that any runs I made in England meant very little to some people, and would continue to do so, unless I produced similar performances at home in New Zealand. Although I always liked to play well in front of the home crowd, I often felt a trifle 'flat' after the strain of a full English season and this factor more than any other sometimes made it hard for me to lift my game at home in New Zealand.'

By the time that Glenn Turner had qualified for Worcestershire, momentous events had taken place in English cricket regarding the registration of overseas players. At a meeting of the registration sub-committee on 3 August 1966, C.G.A. Paris, soon to be the first chairman of the TCCB, announced that Nottinghamshire had written to MCC and all first-class counties suggesting that each county be allowed to register an overseas player without the necessity of a qualification. This suggestion allied to the two Clark reports which had been produced as the result of an enquiry into the state of cricket brought about radical changes in the game. Sunday play was introduced, and in 1969 the John Player League came into being. This was followed in 1972 by the Benson and Hedges Cup, and the administrators of the game became suddenly aware of the need for entertainment, sponsorship, television coverage and effective public relations. Perhaps the most significant and radical change of all was that, from the 1968 season onwards, counties were allowed to recruit one overseas player by immediate registration.

This brought about a fundamental change in the status of the overseas player in county cricket. From Trott, Tarrant and Marshal to Greig, Younis and Turner, he had been, for the most part, a cricketer who had come to England in order to try to earn a living by playing the game he loved. He had come, often at his own expense, in search of work. Now he did not come seeking; he was one who was sought, a star name, a box-office attraction.

Notts had followed up their earlier suggestion with another proposal at the beginning of 1967. This was an amendment to Note ii of Rule 5(d) which they now wanted to read:

> No county shall have more than two Cricketers born overseas on their list of Registered Cricketers in any one season, 'but a player qualified under the Immediate Registration Rule (Rule 9) shall not count as an overseas player for the purpose of this note'.

When the immediate registration of overseas-born cricketers had first been mooted as early as 1965 the Registration Committee had suggested that if such a rule was introduced, players registered under this rule should be supernumary to the existing limit of two overseas-born cricketers per county. When the rule had come close to reality in October 1966, however, the registration committee had recommended that the limit of two overseas players per county should be retained and should include any cricketer on immediate registration. In November 1966 Nottinghamshire had proposed an amendment to allow *four* overseas-born cricketers to each county, but this had gained little support, and the proposal had been withdrawn. A large majority of the registration committee decided that the existing limit of two should be retained 'as being in the long term interest of English cricket'.

This was to become 'a custom more honoured in the breach than the observance'.

On 8 October 1969, the limit of two overseas born cricketers per county was retained subject to the over-riding discretion of the registration sub-committee to increase the number in exceptional circumstances. 'The five year residential period to permit exclusion from this limit of two, no longer referred to the five immediately preceding years, but could be at any time in the Cricketer's life.'

It was also agreed at that time that, under the existing circumstances, cricketers who paid income tax in the United Kingdom should be considered to be resident.

The debate on the place of overseas cricketers in county cricket occupied many in the months before the immediate registration rule came into being in 1968. 'Felix' in *The Cricketer* lamented in May 1967, 'If the nurseries of England were stocked with talented players, there would be no need to import established players from abroad. Indeed, it might be a disservice to the game at home to do so, for young English cricketers might be discouraged or deprived of opportunity and experience. This is scarcely the situation today and the decision of the counties to make overseas players wait a year is a senseless compromise.'

Welcoming the 1968 season, John Arlott greeted the immediate registration rule with joy, balanced by his usual sound reasoning. He thought that the relaxation in the registration rule 'must be basically good for our cricket because, at its lowest, it admits sixteen Test class players in place of the weakest member of each team'. What he did point out was that there was no glut of talent from which the counties could recruit. Clive Lloyd and Greg Chappell were as yet unproved. The leading South Africans, the Pollocks, Barlow and Lindsay, had attractive careers in their own country, and the leading New Zealand, Indian and Pakistani players 'are not so good as our best'. Arlott reasoned also that the employers were in a strong position, since 'between May and September, professional cricket is only available in England'. That has remained a decisive factor, one which has drawn top players to this country in never decreasing numbers.

The opportunity for immediate registration took some counties by surprise. Only eleven of the seventeen availed themselves of the use of the ruling, and of those, Essex, Hampshire, Somerset and Warwickshire were unable to complete their negotiations with players until close to the beginning of the season. Yorkshire, who supported the new legislation in principle, affirmed their policy of playing only those born within the county. They were rewarded by winning the championship in 1968 for the third year in succession, but they have not done so since and, while adhering admirably to their principles, they have suffered many trials and tribulations in the past few years as their supporters have grown restless at the success of others.

The ruling on immediate registration stipulated that a county must offer the overseas cricketer a three-year contract, and this is one factor that could have made some counties wary of approaching a player who might appear to have immense potential in his own country, but was of unknown quality in the exacting programme of six-days-a-week cricket. Several counties, too, laboured under archaic administration, and still do. They were slow to realise the significance of what was happening in the game and the part that overseas cricketers would play in the changing structure, which was soon to see counties competing for four titles, and grounds groaning under capacity crowds on Sunday afternoons and at one-day knock-out cup matches. There were also financial considerations, for it was unlikely that some of the poorer counties, like Essex or Derbyshire, could compete in terms of inducements with the likes of Lancashire or Warwickshire.

Nottinghamshire, who motivated the whole scheme on immediate registration, captured the first prize when they signed Gary Sobers, the undisputed king of cricket at the time. Warwickshire added Rohan Kanhai to their staff, and Gloucestershire lured back Mike Procter. Barry Richards, who had declined to qualify for Gloucestershire by residence after his one game for them in 1965, signed for Hampshire. Lancashire gave immediate registration to the Indian wicket-keeper Engineer and, at the same time, set Clive Lloyd on the path to the one-year period of residential qualification. Sussex took on the West Indian opening batsman Geoff Greenidge, and Kent contracted the exciting Pakistani all-rounder Asif Iqbal. Essex, Glamorgan, Somerset and Worcestershire engaged the lesser known talents of Lee Irvine, Majid Khan, Greg Chappell and Vanburn Holder. Northants had been forced to give immediate registration to Ackerman after he had violated his period of residence by outstaying his leave in South Africa.

It would be wrong to imagine that all these signings were the result of calculated policy decisions. Several counties had yet to work out the needs of limited-over cricket or to foresee the effect that it would have on the game as a whole. There was always the conflict of whether to sign the player that would provide the balance needed in the side or the personality that would attract members and support. The two things have not always been compatible. Commitment, attitude, sociability, respect for captain and colleagues were, as some found to their cost, qualities which could only be proved by a season with the county. Often the mistakes could be on both sides. Certainly this had been the case with Roy Gilchrist, who played thirteen Tests for the West Indies in the late fifties, was as fast as any bowler in the world, but was virtually banned from Test cricket at the age of 24 and went into the Central Lancashire League where he struck terror into many hearts.

Gilchrist came to England in 1957 with a West Indian side that was well beaten, but he was very successful against Pakistan and in India where, after a succession of bouncers and beamers and other misdemeanours, he was sent home in disgrace half-way through a tour on which he had taken 71 wickets at little more than 13 runs each. C.L.R. James and Frank Worrell spoke on his behalf, but the white West Indian captaincy of Goddard and Alexander wanted none of him. In spite of public protest, he remained unforgiven. As James Coldham wrote, 'He seemed to attract conflict and abuse, even in the Lancashire League, where he took hundreds of wickets and numerous hat-tricks.'

Gilchrist was from a poor background in Jamaica. He was a 'natural' fast bowler who arrived in England in 1957 untutored and barely literate. That his talent was ultimately wasted was due in some part to flaws in his own character, but also to a lack of sympathy and understanding by some in positions of authority. Perhaps there have been no other cases of such magnitude with overseas players in English cricket, but that there have been unforeseen problems is undeniable.

Glamorgan won the county championship in 1969. They had three overseas cricketers in the side: the South African Peter Walker, who had qualified by residence and was later to play for England, Pakistani Test cricketer Majid Khan, and West Indian opening batsman Bryan Davis, who qualified by residence in time to play in the 1969 season. Walker, like the West Indian Cordle who was also in the side, had qualified some years earlier, and Cordle, like Walker, effectively became 'Welsh'.

Tony Lewis, the Glamorgan captain in the championship year, comments on the signing of Majid: 'Without any particular planning we struck lucky. Majid Khan had belted an amazing 147 not out against us at Swansea the year before, but who could tell from this slogging innings that he would be technically sound enough to be consistent in the county championship? Majid was 21. The other overseas signing, who had qualified by a year's residence, Bryan Davis from Trinidad, was 27. He had opened the batting four times for West Indies against Australia in 1964. Glamorgan made an early error. They put these two in the same twin-bedded digs in Cardiff without it occurring to anyone that a devout young Muslim, kneeling to recite the Koran, might not fit the domestic habits of a Trinidadian who preferred cola with his rum and some bubbling social life. It took some time for this difficulty to come out. I only mention it because it was probably being experienced by other county clubs at the time.'

Lewis emphasises that in spite of Davis, Majid, Walker, who had in fact been born in Bristol but brought up in Johannesburg, and Cordle, who had settled in Cardiff in his 'teens, the Glamorgan side retained an essential Welshness which gave it identity. He was insistent that the county should not become 'just another professional organisation toiling with a bunch of mercenaries in a commercial league'.

As a captain, he was presented with a different problem in the championship year, and it concerned one of his imported players. 'As a cricketer, Majid settled immediately to confirm his class, but Bryan Davis, opening with Alan Jones, appeared to be unused to the ball moving a lot off the seam. His backward defensive stroke was played with open chest, feet facing to mid-off. Movement late off the pitch often beat him. Half-way through his second season I decided to move him down to number five. He was a little resentful. Firstly it was a tumble of ego for a Test player, especially one who had come to county cricket hoping to re-establish his chances with the West Indian selectors. Relegation in Glamorgan meant diminishing chances back home. These were tough days for the overseas players. They had come as glamour boys to be the stars, and they felt the sceptics chirping at them when they failed.'

The most glamorous of the importations was unquestionably Gary Sobers. He was named as captain of Notts straight away and led the side until 1971, and again in 1973, after which he played one more season of county cricket. Notts climbed to fourth in the championship in 1968, the highest position for 36 years, and they were eighth in 1969, but thereafter they were never in the top ten. They were bottom in 1973 and fifteenth in 1974, Sobers's last year. His impact in the one-day game was equally disappointing. Notts reached the semi-final of the Gillette Cup in 1969 and the quarter-final of the Benson and Hedges Cup in 1973, but, with Sobers, tenth was their highest spot in the Sunday League. As many counties were to learn, one player cannot achieve all on his own, but nevertheless Notts's record under Sobers is not an impressive one, particularly after the first flush of excitement at his arrival had dwindled.

Of his first season with Notts, *Wisden* wrote with enthusiasm: 'Nottinghamshire cricket gained a tremendous boost from the introduction of Garfield Sobers.' 'From the struggling team of recent years they were rejuvenated.' 'Throughout a hard season, his enthusiasm remained undimmed and he was always ready to gamble to keep a game alive. He played many great innings, but his outstanding feat was the world record of six 6's in an over from Nash, the Glamorgan bowler, at Swansea; his 105 not out against Kent at Dover was the fastest century of the season, scored in 77 minutes.'

That promise was never realised, and the euphoria subsided so that the epitaph on his final season was less than ecstatic. 'At the end of the summer Sobers departed the scene. His last season with the club was on a par with the others. There were magical moments; the outstanding memory being his century in eighty-three minutes against Derbyshire at Ilkeston which in the out-come turned out to be the fastest of the season and won him the Lawrence Trophy, as well as the National Sporting Club's prize. It remained a strange fact that in the county championship Sobers never did himself justice. Playing Test cricket he was always able to raise his performance but, regrettably for Nottinghamshire, members saw too few glimpses of the great all-rounder. True, over the last two seasons the demands of every-day cricket im-posed an ever-increasing strain and more injury problems for Sobers.'

Sobers was well liked on the county circuit and popular among spectators for his modesty as well as his outstanding ability, but he had tasted life at the top, and the hard work of seven-days-a-week cricket appeared less and less romantic and attractive as the years passed. England is the only country where one first-class match follows on from another, where there is no week's rest in which a player can find lost form in the nets or lost appetite on the beach.

Nottinghamshire attempted to have Sobers classified as a 'home' player in 1971, thus leaving them at liberty to sign another cricketer on immediate registration. The registration sub-committee informed the county that to establish a residential qualification Sobers would have to reside in the county for the whole of one winter. Alternatively, if he was required by West Indies for a Test series, it might be possible to establish a residential qualification for part of a winter if the county gave advance notice of the fact.

The willingness of the authorities to allow a player to appear in Test matches during his period of qualification was a far cry from what Tarrant and even Roy Marshall had experienced, and in 1968, the counties agreed to encourage overseas players on their books to accept the whole of an England tour if selected by their country.

What Sobers's years with Notts proved was that a cricketer, however good, cannot transform the fortunes of a side on his own, particularly if he is under constant demand at the highest level and is threatened by weariness for endless Test series. As we shall see, the most successful overseas players in county cricket have been those who, for one reason or another, have been able to give total commitment to their side.

Somerset were particularly unlucky in that neither Greg Chappell nor Kerry O'Keefe completed their contracts with the county. They also attempted to obtain the services of John Inverarity through residential qualification from 8 April 1968, for he was teaching at Millfield School, but he was selected for the Australian side which came to England that year and eventually failed to complete his qualification period.

Chappell was signed on immediate registration for the 1968 season. He had made his debut for South Australia in 1966-67 at the age of eighteen and was considered a most promising young batsman, and that promise was confirmed the following season. It was, however, a gamble on the part of Somerset to sign him. Although his elder brother Ian was in the Australian side, Greg was little known and he was not a Test cricketer. His international debut was to come in 1970-71 after his two seasons in England. He scored 1,163 runs and took 26 wickets with his medium pace in his first season, when, in *Wisden*'s words, he 'found life on wet pitches a trial, but adapted himself well to the firmer pitches of late summer'. The following season he hit 1,330 runs and took 45 wickets. His stroke play was majestic, and he hit the first century to be recorded in the John Player League. He aspired to Test cricket, however, and he informed the county at the end of the 1969 season that he would not be returning to fulfil the last year of his contract.

In effect, eighteen months' continuous play had sated Chappell's appetite for cricket. He had found his county motivation waning. On his own admission, he was learning bad habits. He was beginning to think that if he did not get runs one day, he would get them the next or the day after. Nor was he to be the last overseas player to reach that state of mind, although he reached it more quickly than most.

It was not just the loss of mental discipline that affected Chappell; it was the self-questioning that attacks us all when we consider the prospect of doing the same job for the next twenty years. In his own words, he felt threatened. He observed his Somerset colleagues and saw them as 'nice blokes, good company, good friends', for whom 'cricket had become a soporific surrogate for employment that might stretch their intellects'. He was confident that a few years of Test cricket would soon be his – many Australian newspapers were shocked that he had not been included in the side for England in 1968 – and that he would be able to play all the cricket that he wanted in, and for, his own country. In truth, he was an intelligent young man, a cricketer of the highest quality, who found that his own background, culture and aspirations were ultimately at variance with the traditions of county cricket, and while he respected those traditions, he no longer wished to be a part of them.

In other cases, it was the county rather than the player who became disillusioned. Alan Connolly was the outstanding bowler of the Australian side in 1968, and it was believed that Middlesex had achieved a great scoop when they signed him in 1969. His fast-medium pace and style seemed ideally suited for English conditions, and he was a warm, likeable and friendly young man. He took 74 wickets in 1969, but his second season was a near disaster. 'His addiction to experiment often proved costly. In the final six matches of the season he did not take more than one wicket in an innings. This, of course, proved particularly disappointing considering his success in the Tests. On the evidence, he was one of those rare types, a Test rather than a county bowler.'

He did not return to complete his contract, retiring from cricket because of a back injury.

At the same time, Middlesex engaged another overseas player by residential qualification, the Rhodesian Norman Featherstone. Middlesex pressed to have Featherstone considered a permanent resident of the United Kingdom so that he could cease to count as one of their overseas-born cricketers, but in view of the fact that he had returned home to South Africa for two winters to see his family and to seek employment, the sub-committee on registration could not accede to Middlesex's request.

Featherstone was another equally charming young man who could bat attractively, but he never seemed to relish the need for consistent application in the county game. He always suggested impatience. He left Middlesex in 1979 and played for Glamorgan for two seasons.

Middlesex were not lucky in their importation ventures before Wayne Daniel joined them in 1977. As we have noted, Connolly was a disappointment and Featherstone failed to live up to expectations. In 1970 they noticed a left-handed batsman, Larry Gomes, who was touring England with the West Indian Schools side. They attempted to sign him, but in August 1971 they informed the TCCB that they had been refused a work permit for Gomes. The government argument was that work permits were only given to *eminent* cricketers from overseas, and Gomes, with no first-class experience at the time of the application and with only four first-class games in the West Indies to his credit by the end of the 1972-73 season, certainly did not fall into that category.

The matter was taken up with the Minister of Sport, and Gomes began residential qualification for Middlesex in 1972. He made his debut for the county in 1973, at the age of nineteen. He played 42 first-class matches for them in three seasons, from 1973 to 1975, and hit only 1,199 runs, at an average of 22.20, and took only 23 wickets at more than 40 runs apiece. However mediocre his record with Middlesex, Gomes had gained invaluable experience. He had joined them a shy, reticent young man who would sit quietly in a corner of the bar after a match, sipping an orange juice, remote from the social intercourse of the two teams. To the astonishment of many, in 1976 he became a Test cricketer, his technique and temperament matured by his years in county cricket which offered him far greater experience than he could find in the West Indies.

The career of Vanburn Holder followed a pattern similar to that of Gomes, although he served his county, Worcestershire, longer – 1968 to 1980 – and better, with more than five hundred wickets. He had played one first-class match and taken one first-class wicket when Tom Graveney spotted him and invited him to join Worcestershire. The county was in need of a fast bowler, and Holder was young, 22, and fitted the bill. Arguably, he would have made his mark in any case, but his development was assured when he joined Worcestershire, and within a year he was a Test match cricketer and one of West Indies' Five Players of the Year.

The planning of Sussex, like that of Middlesex, was ill-fated and ill-conceived. Geoff Greenidge was their immediate registration signing. He had 265 first-class runs and eight first-class wickets to his credit when Sussex engaged him, and 205 of his runs had come in one innings for Barbados against Jamaica, in 1966-67. This was, in fact, to be the only double century of his career, and although he played for Sussex until 1975, he averaged under 29 in his 152 matches and ceased to bowl. He played five Tests for West Indies between 1971 and 1973, and he went with D.H. Robins's XI to South Africa, an action which caused his country, Barbados, to be refused entry into Guyana for a Shell

Shield match because he was in the side. His record for Sussex was that of an average, perhaps even below average, county opener, and as was remarked, there is little purpose in importing a player who can provide only the mediocrity which you can obtain from a home-grown player at half the price.

The Sussex dilemma was sharpened by the case of Solkar, a very useful all-rounder who played 27 Tests for India. He was recommended to the county by their former player the Nawab of Pataudi, junior. He played against the New Zealand tourists in 1969 and was said to be qualifying. On 27 July 1970 it was agreed by the registration sub-committee that he should be allowed home to play in the winter. At the same meeting, permission was also granted to Joshi, also of Sussex, and to Bernard Julien of Kent. On 5 June 1972 it was agreed that Solkar had violated his residential qualification by not returning, and his game against the New Zealanders remained the extent of his first-class career with Sussex.

Meanwhile Sussex had engaged Udaykumar Joshi, so giving them their quota of two specially registered players. Joshi, an off-break bowler, first appeared for Saurashtra in the Ranji Trophy in 1965 and took a wicket with his first ball in first-class cricket. In his first season with Sussex, 1971, he took 74 wickets, but thereafter his number of wickets declined as their cost increased. His contract was not renewed after 1974, nor did he ever play in Test cricket.

The Sussex choice of overseas players was prompted by their economic position at the time. They certainly could not have afforded the wages of a Clive Lloyd or a Mike Procter, and they made the fatal mistake of looking for success on the cheap. Dilip Doshi, later of Notts and Warwickshire, played for their second eleven, as did Ken McEwan. McEwan had come to Sussex at Greig's invitation, but although McEwan showed enough class for Sussex second eleven to excite the interest of so perceptive a judge as Doug Insole, when the player approached the committee and asked if they were prepared to offer him a contract, he was told, in an evasive way, that they were really interested in signing an Indian cricketer. For Sussex, the rejection was a disaster; for Essex, it proved to be the beginning of a golden age.

Alongside the flounderings of Sussex and Middlesex, short-sighted and ill-judged investments based on a false economy, were the calculated policies of Lancashire and Warwickshire.

For Lancashire, 1968 was one of the most significant years in their history. Lean years had brought dwindling gate receipts and a decline in membership. The signing of Ramadhin had come too late and been a failure, and the committee were aware that only success on the field could rid the club of the apathy which engulfed it.

The committee itself had undergone changes. One of the most trenchant critics of the old committee, Cedric Rhoades, was the most energetic of new members. His total commitment to the cause of Lancashire cricket soon saw him elected Vice-Chairman, and then as Chairman he began to rejuvenate the club. He was a staunch ally of the new captain, Jack Bond, and together they restored faith in Lancashire cricket, with the considerable aid of two importations.

The record books will show Bond was a modest performer with the bat; what they will not show is that he was an inspiring leader, a most brilliant fielder and one of the first to realise the challenge and rewards offered by the one-day game. Of the side that Bond led in 1968, only Pullar, Higgs and Statham were capped players of long standing, and all three were to leave the county within eighteen months. David Lloyd, Wood, Shuttleworth and Engineer were capped in 1968, and Clive Lloyd and Sullivan were capped the following year, when Jack Simmons began to win a regular place in the side.

The signing of Farokh Engineer on immediate registration in 1968 was an inspired act on the part of the Lancashire administration. It showed a true assessment of the needs of the county, and it showed that those responsible had done their homework, something which few others had done.

There was an air of surprise that Lancashire had imported Engineer. He was, after all, a wicket-keeper, and all counties are usually capable of finding a wicket-keeper of adequate ability without having to resort to importation. But not only was Engineer a very fine Test wicket-keeper, he was also an unortho-dox, aggressive batsman who could give the side an ebullient start when he opened the innings.

Engineer had been in the Indian Test side since 1961 and had excited people on the tour of England in 1967, but, as a batsman, he disappointed in his first season for Lancashire. As a wicket-keeper, however, he was an exotic extrovert, the enthusiastic pivot of all that went on in the field, and from the moment of his arrival, and with the inspiration of Bond's leadership, Lancashire became the most exciting fielding side in the country. There was a panache about Engineer's wicket-keeping which warmed the spectator, and he threatened batsmen with his zest.

By 1969 Clive Lloyd had qualified through residence, and Rhoades and Bond had completed the jigsaw that would bring the crowds flocking back to Old Trafford and send the membership soaring again. Lloyd was known to Lancastrians, for he had played with Haslingden in the Lancashire League and was the only batsman in the League to top a thousand runs in 1968. He had played his first Test match in December 1966, and the following season had hit two centuries against England, but when Lancashire invited him to qualify he was still something of an unknown quantity, although his fielding in the covers had already won the highest accolades.

The Lancashire planning had its immediate reward. In 1968 they leapt to sixth in the championship, and in 1969 they became the first winners of the John Player League, retaining the title the following season. They won the Gillette Cup three years in succession, from 1970 to 1972, and they were beaten finalists in 1974 and 1976, before taking the cup again in 1975. These were the most glorious years of Lancashire cricket since McDonald and the 1920s.

The triumphs were essentially a team effort, shaped by Bond, but with Engineer and Lloyd providing the character and personality which had been so sadly missing for two decades. The strength was that neither Engineer nor Lloyd was ever considered as an outsider, a bird of passage. Both settled in Lancashire and engaged in business there. Both were embraced by the local community as Lancastrians. Engineer, after his poor start with the bat, became immensely popular. He chatted to everyone. He was always eager and cheerful. Instinctively he knew that the essential character of county cricket was that those in the seats should be able to identify with those on the field. Clive Lloyd was equally approachable. He was 25 when he began his career with Lancashire, an exciting new cricketer who enjoyed his cricket and wanted the crowd to enjoy it with him.

In 1974 Lloyd became captain of the West Indies, a commitment which brought demands that could not always be reconciled with county continuity. In 1976 Lloyd was not available because he was leading West Indies against England, and the following year he played only three matches because of injury. By then, Engineer had gone, establishing a successful business career in Manchester after twenty years at the top in international cricket. To the end he retained what John Kay described as 'that inconsistent streak which made him such an entertaining player'.

On Lloyd's recommendation, Lancashire signed the West Indian fast bowler, Colin Croft, in 1978. This was as disastrous a move as the signing of Engineer and Lloyd had been successful. Croft was at the beginning of what promised to be a highly successful Test cricket. He was fast and dangerous, but he proved to have neither the discipline nor the temperamental stability needed for a county career. His petulant and disgraceful behaviour when he barged the umpire in a Test match in New Zealand, and his stream of bouncers against the Australian side touring the West Indies in 1978, served only to support this view.

When Engineer played his last game in 1976 a golden period of Lancashire cricket came to an end, and by the time Clive Lloyd was given the job of trying to resuscitate it, it was too late.

The Warwickshire policy followed similar lines to that of Lancashire, although it was motivated by the personal ambition of a wealthy man who has given much to cricket, Derrick Robins, and the energy of one of county cricket's best chairmen, Cyril Goodway.

Robins passionately wanted Warwickshire to win the championship, and the immediate registration rule gave an opportunity to build the side that could accomplish this. Lance Gibbs began a residential qualification in 1967 so that he was available for the county championship in 1968. He was already a most accomplished Test cricketer of eleven years' standing and had played in the Lancashire League. He was joined in the Warwickshire side in 1968 by his West Indian team-mate, Rohan Kanhai.

Kanhai had played in the leagues in Scotland and Lancashire, but Warwickshire had long nursed an interest in him. They had not approached him earlier because their first aim had been to sign the South African all-rounder, Eddie Barlow. Barlow refused all inducements to come to play in England, so the Warwickshire Committee again turned their attentions to Kanhai.

A.C. Smith, the Warwickshire captain, had gone to Jamaica in February, 1968, to look at another West Indian cricketer, but he reported back unfavourably, although this player was later to sign for another county. Smith was then advised to look at other players, and he concurred with the recommendations of Gibbs and David Brown, who, like Kanhai, were engaged in the England–West Indies Test series at the time, and suggested that Kanhai was the man Warwickshire should sign. In March 1968 he signed a three-year contract for the Midland county. In fact, he was to play for them until 1977.

In his wonderful history of Warwickshire, Leslie Duckworth pays the warmest of tributes to Kanhai, and it is one worth recalling every time the importation of overseas players is heavily criticised.

'I shall always feel a personal debt of gratitude to Warwickshire for engaging him, not so much because of the runs he has scored for them, though they have been entertaining enough in all conscience, but because I was able to see again in him what batsmen were like in the days when they still believed it was their main function in life to hit the ball hard – plus, of course, the personal panache he brought to the game. Sometimes he would let quite hittable balls pass him for no apparent reason, but then the tiger that always lurked beneath that seemingly benign exterior would stir and pounce and you would see a cut of blinding brilliance, or a drive that would make you instinctively draw your hand away from even the thought that you might be called upon to stop it. He was sometimes a man of moods – aren't we all? – but he let the younger generation of Warwickshire players and spectators see what real batsmanship could be, and I knew that I had not dreamed there were really such batsmen once.

For that I shall be eternally grateful.'

On 1 December 1970, Warwickshire brought to the notice of the registration sub-committee that Kanhai had been living in England for more than five years, and that he now had a home in Blackpool. The county's point was accepted, and Kanhai was no longer regarded as an Immediate Registration, so making it possible for Warwickshire to obtain the services of another overseas cricketer on a residential qualification.

Kanhai recommended that his county should try to obtain a young elegant left-hander, Alvin Kallicharran, who was to make his Test debut in April 1972 when he hit a century against New Zealand. Another important recommendation came from Derrick Robins who was on holiday in Barbados and saw Kallicharran play. Alan Smith flew out to the West Indies and signed Kallicharran in face of strong competition from other counties.

Kallicharran was offered a three-year contract, and it is interesting to note that although Middlesex had experienced difficulty in obtaining a work permit for Gomes, Warwickshire experienced none in obtaining one for Kallicharran. When this matter was discussed in August 1971, the TCCB believed that the *eminence* of the cricketer concerned had probably been determined by the length of contract that he was offered.

A fourth West Indian Test player was added to the staff at Edgbaston in 1972 when wicket-keeper Deryck Murray was signed on special registration. Murray was up at Cambridge University in 1965 and 1966, when he led the side, but, as was commented wryly, he was more successful on the cricket field than he was in the examination room. While at Cambridge he was registered to play for Nottinghamshire – it had always been allowable for cricketers engaged in a course of study to assist a county in the vacation period – and in December 1966 Notts gained a two-year extension to his registration, for he had now moved to the University of Nottingham. In 1968 it was decided that he was considered to have commenced residence in January 1964, in spite of the time he had spent at university, and he played for Nottinghamshire until 1969.

In 1972 he was given special and immediate registration for Warwickshire because he had not played for his previous county for three years and was not registered with them. Since he had been a registered county cricketer before 1971, it was decided that his registration by Warwickshire did not unbalance their quota of overseas players. At the same Registration sub-committee meeting, in February 1972, it was stated that the 'ultimate aim of allowing only two overseas-born cricketers to be registered' was the policy. Warwickshire now had *four* West Indian Test players in their side and also had the Pakistani Ibadulla on their staff.

As with Lancashire, Warwickshire's policy on importations brought immediate results. In 1968, with Gibbs, Kanhai and Ibadulla in the side, they won the Gillette Cup. In 1971 they were pipped for the championship by Surrey, who lost fewer matches. The following season, with Kallicharran and Murray boosting the side, they were champions. Success had been bought, and an ambition had been realised.

PART 5
The Price

Legislation is often an attempt to clarify something that is already taking place, or to respond to a social demand or need. So it is with cricket. The advent of the limited-over game had stimulated a new interest in the game as a whole. It was necessary that this interest be maintained, and that could only be done by providing those who paid to watch the game with quality and excitement in both personality and performance. If the personality and performance could not be provided by the home-grown cricketer, then the county must look overseas, where there were players whose names and origins were surrounded with a romanticism which gave them an attraction. There were thousands of people to whom Sobers had long been a distant, revered figure, but who were now able to take a bus or train to a county ground and watch him play. There were followers of the game who had read that Barry Richards was the greatest batsman in the world, but who had believed that he would remain forever a legend of whom they would only read; now it was possible to watch him bat for Hampshire.

Allied to this desire for colour and quality was the growing demand for success which we have already mentioned. It is the biggest single factor which distinguishes the way the game is followed today from the way in which it was followed in the 1930s, when people certainly longed for their counties to be victorious, but still followed them when they were not. In the early 1980s, a county secretary could say to the present writer at the beginning of a season, 'We are in a state of rebuilding, and we know that we are not going to win anything this year. We know also that that will cost us two thousand members.'

This need for success has imposed upon counties an urgency

to strengthen their sides with overseas players. They argued that they were compensating for the lack of talent to be found at home, but, in truth, that talent was not always lacking. It was simply that the demand for success created an impatience for instant glory which hindered the development of several young players and sometimes meant the end of a cricketing career before it had really started.

Northamptonshire have an uneasy and inconsistent record with regard to overseas players. Ackerman's violation of his residential qualification had caused them to use the Immediate Registration rules to qualify him. After three seasons, in spite of the county's efforts to change his qualification to residential, he returned to South Africa. Meanwhile Mushtaq Mohammad had integrated well and gave Northants excellent service as an all-rounder. He played for them until 1977 and captained the side for several seasons.

Sarfraz Nawaz, however, presented different problems. He began residential qualification for the county in 1969 and played in the championship in 1970. In 1971 he was with the Pakistan touring side, was injured and showed little enthusiasm for playing for Northants, with the result that he was not retained. He joined Nelson in the Lancashire League, where he learned much, and in 1974 he was re-engaged by Northants although he could only play for half a season because of his commitments with the Pakistan side. In 1975, however, he was an outstanding success in county cricket and was one of only two bowlers to take a hundred wickets in the season. He assisted Northants until 1982, and shared in two cup triumphs with them.

When Sarfraz was not retained at the end of the 1971 season and Ackerman returned to South Africa, Northants were confronted with a problem. The county had been playing dull cricket and had been floundering in the lower half of the championship table as well as achieving nothing in the one-day competitions. The committee reacted by signing Bishen Bedi, one of the greatest of slow left-arm bowlers, on immediate registration. Cottam and Dye were also added to the attack, and Northants climbed to fourth in the championship and won the Gillette Cup in 1976.

Bedi was a most popular acquisition. He has always been quick to acknowledge the debt that he owes to Northants, and to accept that being involved in cricket seven days a week enabled him to develop as a bowler and as a person. He was sensitive enough to be aware of the challenge that county cricket presented. 'It's very hard to get accepted in an English dressing-room; the average pro takes a long time to loosen up, and you have to have a considerable personal success before you really become part of the team.' He asserted that his time with Northants improved his application and powers of concentration although, to the spectator, those appeared to be qualities with which he was born. He had a wonderful control of flight, delivering the ball from a variety of heights, but disguising the point of delivery with a subtlety that confused batsmen. To watch him bowl was an aesthetic pleasure, and the crowds loved his artistry, cunning and good humour. Twice he reached a hundred wickets in a season in his years with Northants, and the county reawakened. But who paid the price?

Three young Northants professionals, Stone, Osman and Watson, might suggest that they did. All three were dismissed at the end of the 1971 season, and Chris Stone is not alone in believing that they were sacked so that Northants could pay Bedi's wages.

Chris Stone was a very promising all-rounder. A right-handed batsman and an off-break bowler, he has become a notable coach and assists Dorset in the holiday period. He feels that the person who had most right to feel aggrieved was Wayne Osman, who has played for Hertfordshire since leaving Northants.

He was 21 years old in 1971 and was just establishing himself in the county side. He made his debut in 1970 and played eight matches the following year, being used with reasonable success as a left-handed opening batsman. In the second eleven he thrived, scoring 640 runs in seventeen innings and growing in confidence with each match. With Ackerman, Prideaux and Kettle leaving the county, he had reason to believe that his opportunities for first team cricket would increase. When he was called to the secretary's office he had no inkling of the news with which he was to be greeted. He was told that his services would no longer be required.

None would argue that Stone, Osman or Watson would have

been as valuable to Northants as Bedi proved to be. Bedi was a great cricketer; the three young players would probably never have been more than good county men. But it is an inescapable fact that the importation of Bedi, as with the importation of any overseas cricketer, cost an English-born cricketer his place in the county side. Fifteen years after the importation of Bedi, Northants were to sign another overseas Test player, Roger Harper, and he was to oust from the county side one who had been spoken of as a future England all-rounder.

On the whole Northants had not been lucky with their overseas cricketers, and undoubtedly the return that they got from Kapil Dev was a bitter disappointment to them. He first came to England with the Indian side 1979. The opening match of the tour was at Northampton, and Kapil Dev hit 102 out of a stand of 143 in 74 minutes. He hit a six and nineteen fours and made a tremendous impression. As he was twenty years old and a fast bowler of outstanding ability, he was recognised as a prime target for a county club.

Kapil Dev chose to play in the Lancashire League and excited people with his performances for Nelson, but Northants persuaded him to sign for them and appear in mid-week matches in 1981. In fact, he played in only three matches, and he made only sixteen appearances for the county in his three seasons as a registered player. He produced some spectacular hitting, the best Northants had seen since the days of Colin Milburn, but he failed to bowl as quickly or as well as the county had hoped. He is a man of great charm and easy good humour, but India lean heavily on him at Test level, for he is unquestionably the one great bowler of pace that the country has produced, and his is a temperament that is not ideally suited to the grind of the county circuit.

What Kapil Dev did not succeed in doing at Northampton was to provide the county with the fast bowler for which they yearned. South Africans Jim Carse and 'Spook' Hanley were others who failed to realise the expectations that the county had of them, but Hanley, in particular, was past his best when Northants signed him.

Still searching for the missing link, Northants signed Roger Harper and Ray Joseph for the 1985 season although they knew that they would not be able to play both players in the same match. Joseph is a fast-medium bowler who has done well for Guyana, but who has not come close to the West Indian Test side owing to the wealth of talent that the selectors have at their disposal. Harper, an off-spin bowler, hard-hitting batsman and brilliant fielder, has won a place in the West Indies team and many see him as a future captain of the Test eleven.

Joseph was released at the end of the 1985 season as Harper was seen to fit smoothly into the Northants side. Harper's contribution to the county's cricket was considerably more than his 763 runs and 58 wickets would suggest. He proved to be totally committed to the side, inspirational in the field and popular with both players and spectators. He bowled more overs in the county championship than any Northants bowler had done for seventeen years. Conversely, Richard Williams bowled half as many overs as he had done in previous seasons.

Richard Williams was born in 1957, made his first-class debut in 1974 and was capped in 1979. An off-break bowler and chunky, attacking batsman, he was very close to selection for the England side that went to the West Indies in 1981. He was still an England candidate at the beginning of the 1984 season and was chosen for the MCC against champion county, Essex. This fixture traditionally heralds the season, and the composition of the MCC side is always viewed with interest as it is believed to reflect the thinking of the Test selectors. Unfortunately, Williams took little part in the match, falling ill and being unable to bowl. Since that point his career has been in decline. He held his place in the Northants side when Harper first arrived, but, in 1986, with Nick Cook added to the staff, his opportunities became restricted. Cook's slow left-arm spin gave the Northants attack greater variety. Williams offered a duplicate of what Roger Harper gave, and Harper was the first choice. Williams played in only four first-class matches in 1986, and only two of them were in the county championship. An all-rounder considered to be of Test potential eighteen months earlier had seen his future in the game threatened by the importation of a West Indian Test player.

From the outset the counties were aware of such problems, but they were in a dilemma. On the one hand, supporters clamoured for stars and success; on the other, there was the need to groom young talent.

As early as May 1969, Mike Turner, the Leicestershire secretary, wrote to the other counties recommending that steps should be taken to prevent the escalation in the number of overseas-born cricketers coming into county cricket. Leicestershire themselves had just obtained the services of Graham McKenzie, the Australian pace bowler, and he and Rhodesian Brian Davison were to help them to their first county championship in 1975 and to a string of successes in the Benson and Hedges Cup and the John Player League. Later, Paddy Clift, another Rhodesian, was added to the Leicestershire staff.

In October 1971 the TCCB required the registration committee to find out the effect on standards of English cricket of the importation of overseas cricketers. The committee produced some startling figures as to the increasing number of importations in county cricket, viz:

$$1966 - 37$$
$$1967 - 39$$
$$1968 - 51$$
$$1969 - 56$$
$$1970 - 56$$
$$1971 - 65$$

They did not feel able to express an expert view, but they considered that the trend over the six seasons of their study would lead to a reduced opportunity for young English cricketers to come into county cricket, and they felt that this could well have an adverse effect on the future standards at international level.

They suggested that the number of overseas-born cricketers entering county cricket in the future should be severely limited, although they accepted that those already registered, contracted or currently qualifying under the existing rules should be unaffected by future legislation. Among their recommendations was the one that a cricketer born overseas was only qualified for England if he had been resident in the British Isles for the preceding ten consecutive years. It was believed that the ultimate aim of all counties was to reduce the number of overseas players to not more than two per county.

While this may have been the ideal at the highest level, at club level the number of overseas cricketers proliferated season by season. The wind of change which had brought in limited-over cricket, immediate registration and a fiercer sense of competitiveness at county level effected changes at club level too. For years the South had stood aloof from the idea of playing for points and trophies at club level, but by the 1970s, sponsored leagues covered the Home Counties and the South Coast. Standards improved and fielding, in particular, reached new heights, but with points, prestige and money at stake, clubs began to take cricket more seriously than they had ever done. Most top clubs had always fielded cricketers who had appeared for county second elevens; now they regularly included two or three overseas players in their sides.

Each summer England swarms with cricketers from the Commonwealth, Sheffield Shield players from Australia and Shell Trophy cricketers from New Zealand anxious to develop their skills in English conditions. Clubs are offered a galaxy of talent, and for every Commonwealth cricketer who is thrust into a first eleven, a young home-born cricketer is frustrated in his ambitions. The desire for success dominates our cricket at every level, and for success a price must be paid.

In 1976 George Murray was in England engaged in a year's educational research. By then in his fifties, Murray had a distinguished record in cricket administration and had played top grade cricket in Victoria. He was later to manage an Australian under-19 side to England. As a coach and an enthusiast for the game, he offered himself to Dulwich. The club welcomed him eagerly, as a player. He was put straight into the first team and helped Dulwich to the final of the Haig National Club Knock-Out Competition at Lord's. Dulwich lost to Scarborough, but George Murray's 55 not out won him the individual award, a bat, which was presented for the best innings of the match. A fine cricketer, he was delighted to have played at Lord's, but he remains puzzled at the English attitude.

'If Len Hutton had come to Australia for a year and offered his services to my club, we'd have said, "Great to see you, Sir Len, you could do a terrific job for us. We've got some promising young lads in the third team. Would you look after them and help to bring them along?" Here you put me in the first team.'

The number of overseas cricketers appearing in matches at a level lower than first-class began to trouble the TCCB, and it was agreed that only one cricketer not qualified for England should be allowed to play in county under-25 and second eleven matches.

Another problem that concerned the TCCB was related to their own ruling on a ten-year residential period of qualification for a cricketer born overseas before he could be considered as English. A move to amend this rule and reduce the period to eight years was rejected in 1972, but exceptions were made for young cricketers who had been born abroad, but who had been brought to England by their parents and settled here. It was decided that any cricketer who had been living in England for four consecutive years since the day before his fourteenth birthday should be considered as being qualified for England. Roland Butcher, Neil Williams, Norman Cowans and Wilf Slack of Middlesex are all covered by this ruling, although Slack, Butcher and Williams have all returned to the Caribbean in the past few years to play in Shell Shield cricket. Butcher and Williams have also played for Tasmania in the Sheffield Shield.

Even the before-the-age-of-fourteen rule did not cover Gladstone Small, and the registration committee had to use their discretionary powers so that he could be registered for Warwickshire in 1979 and be considered eligible for England in 1981. The youngest of a large family, Small had arrived in England in 1977 shortly after his sixteenth birthday. Under the existing rules, he would not be qualified to play for England until 16 September 1987, but it was argued that his father had been in this country since 1961 and that, but for lack of money, he would have brought Gladstone to England some years earlier. The young man had learned most of his cricket in Birmingham, had played for Warwickshire Schools and Young Amateurs, and had been selected for the England Schools side but had been unable to play. It was further argued that, although he was qualified by birth to play for West Indies, he would choose to play for England. The registration committee agreed with the arguments put forward, and the ICC was approached and approved that Small be registered under the four-year rule and be considered eligible for England as from 16 September 1981.

It was, of course, important to a county that any cricketer who was qualified as eligible for England should be recognised as such. The whole question of registration had plagued the administrators, and they had begun a complete review of the matter at the beginning of 1974. The regulations formulating the restriction on the number of overseas cricketers were announced in January 1979.

1. For the seasons 1979, 1980 and 1981 – each county will be allowed to play two 'non-qualified for England' cricketers, irrespective of whether or not they were registered (or negotiations were in progress) prior to 28 November 1978.
2. From season 1982 onwards, a county may only play two such cricketers in a match if both of them were registered (or negotiations were in progress) prior to 28 November 1978. Otherwise they may only play one such cricketer.

An exception was made in the case of Gloucestershire, who were allowed to continue to play their three contracted overseas players for the time being.

These restrictions, which effectively would reduce the number of overseas cricketers in county cricket to sixteen within a few years, made it imperative that counties took advantage of those regulations which allowed them to consider some of their players born overseas as *English*. In particular the counties, and seemingly the England selectors, were anxious to exploit the rule which allowed that a cricketer whose father or mother had been born in the British Isles and who himself had lived in this country for four consecutive years should be considered eligible for England even though he had been born and had played abroad.

It was, of course, this rule which allowed the South African-born Chris Smith and Allan Lamb to play for England, paradoxically at a time when English-born players like Gooch, Emburey and Taylor were banned from the England side for having played for an 'England XI' in South Africa.

Lamb hit three centuries against West Indies in the Test series of 1984 and followed it with a fourth hundred against Sri Lanka, but he remains hurt that, in spite of that outstanding perform-ance, 'I was still the interloper, the South African who had sneaked into the England side before the Test and County Cricket Board had time to close the door in their qualification laws, just because the gateway into the Test arena I would nor-mally have taken had been closed to me as a result of the world's abhorrence of the apartheid system in the country of my birth.' At least, as Lamb pointed out, he had to serve a period of qualifica-tion, settling in England and making friends, whereas the athlete Zola Budd was given instant nationality so that she could compete in the Olympic Games, one of the greatest disservices the British Government and those who administer athletics in Britain have done for a person and the sport.

Those who see the acceptance of becoming qualified for Eng-land as an easy option for a cricketer born overseas are insensitive to the problems and conflicts that can beset him. Gehan Mendis was born in Colombo and educated at St Thomas College. He came to England at the age of fourteen in 1969 and completed his education at Brighton, Hove and Sussex Grammar School. At sixteen, he played for Sussex second eleven, and later he trained as a teacher at Bede College, Durham University. In June 1972 Sussex applied for him to be considered as qualified to play for England, but the ten-year residential period was insisted upon.

Mendis has consistently been mentioned as a prospective Eng-land opener, and certainly he would have been a graceful addition to the Test arena. In 1982 the country of his birth, Sri Lanka, achieved Test status, and later, when visiting relations, Mendis was approached with a view to his making himself available for selection for the Sri Lankan side. If he had accepted the oppor-tunity, he would, of course, have violated his 'qualified for Eng-land' status, so reluctantly he declined. It could not have been easy for a likeable and ambitious young man to decide to turn his back on the chance of a Test career, but he believed that he had made his decision some years earlier when he had elected to follow the career of a professional cricketer in England.

Mendis left Sussex for Lancashire in 1986, a year which saw Rodney Ontong forced to make a similar decision. Ontong was not deemed as having qualified to be available for England until the completion of his ten-year residential period in 1981. He had continued to play in the Currie Cup and Castle Bowl in South Africa, the country of his birth, and in 1985-86, he was considered to be the best off-spinner in the Republic. It was stated that he was likely to be chosen to play for South Africa against Kim Hughes's Australian side, but he was informed by the TCCB that, if he did so, he would be considered to have violated his qualification and would be reclassified as an overseas player. He then declared himself unavailable for the South African side, but did point out that the TCCB's stipulation was rather harsh in view of the fact that the South Africa–'Australia' series was not recognised by the ICC.

Neal Radford almost suffered a grave setback to his qualification plans when he appeared for a South African under-25 XI in the 1981-82 season. Born in Zambia, Radford had had doubts cast upon his qualification to play for England throughout 1981, but it was finally accepted in the September of that year that he would be eligible to play for England from the beginning of the 1983 season. When it was learned, in April 1982, that he had played for a South African side in what was believed to be a representative game concern was expressed, but Radford survived, became recognised as English, and although he was not re-engaged by Lancashire, the county who had pressed for his qualification, he ultimately found fame and a Test place when he moved to Worcestershire.

While the majority of cricketers who have had the opportunity to qualify for eligibility for England have chosen to take it, there have been exceptions, the most notable of whom is Gordon Greenidge. Greenidge was born in Barbados, where he was brought up by his grandmother, his mother having followed his father to England to seek work. The boy came to this country before his fourteenth birthday, went to school in Reading and represented Berkshire Schools. By the time he was eighteen, like Slack, Butcher and Cowans, he was eligible to play for England.

Greenidge had not done particularly well with Berkshire Schools, but he was approached by both Hampshire and Warwickshire, and he chose to join the county closest to his home, where he was greatly helped by coach Arthur Holt. He made his first-class debut for Hampshire in 1970 and began his profitable opening partnership with the South African Barry Richards. He passed a thousand runs for the first time in 1971 and was capped the following season. His significant advance was noticed by the West Indian authorities, and he was invited to return to Barbados to assist the island in the Shell Shield in 1982-83.

As he had learned his cricket in England, played two and a half seasons for Hampshire and been a capped player before he appeared in first-class cricket in the West Indies, it was hoped that Greenidge would opt to play for England if selected. This hope was strengthened when Ron Headley was chosen ahead of him for the West Indies side that toured England in 1973. Greenidge has never disguised his disappointment at not being selected for that tour, and he contemplated being prepared to play for England, but when he was sounded on the point by Charles Knott, chairman of the Hampshire Cricket Committee, he replied that he wished to wait a little longer to see if West Indies would select him. In November 1974 he made his Test debut for West Indies against India, at Bangalore. Viv Richards made his test debut in the same match. Greenidge was run out for 93 in his first innings and hit 107 in the second. It was the beginning of an illustrious Test career.

To determine the reasons for Greenidge wishing to remain qualified for West Indies when his cricketing experiences seemed to point towards him becoming recognised as an England player is not easy, but the writings which have appeared under his name give some hint. When he went to school in Reading at the age of fourteen the depth of racial hatred that he encountered was far greater than he had been taught to expect when, in Barbados, he was told of the anti-black feeling he might meet in England. In his own words, he was 'lonely, bewildered and overwhelmed with the size of everything'. He suffered because of his thick Barbadian accent; ironically, later, after years in Hampshire, he was to be dubbed 'the Englishman' in the West Indian side because of the way in which he spoke.

It would be idle to believe that the scars from the wounds suffered in those early years at school in England disappeared immediately he began to play county cricket. He thought of himself as West Indian. He was aware of West Indian history, and he was concerned for the dignity of the black man and the need for the West Indians to retain their separate culture. England's loss was West Indies' gain, for few batsmen have produced such consistently exhilarating displays at international level. The loss has also been Hampshire's, for had Greenidge opted to play for England in 1973 or 1974, they would have been able to register another overseas-born cricketer.

The restrictions on overseas players have led counties to attempt to circumnavigate the problem in an effort to strengthen their sides. The best ally that they discovered in their efforts was the Treaty of Rome.

The first ICC Trophy tournament in 1979 brought to the attention of the cricket world the high standard of play that had been reached in many of the associate member countries. Once again Zimbabwe proved the strongest side, but the performance of Denmark, and particularly of their fast bowler Ole Mortensen, won much praise. Six foot three inches tall, 21 years old, Mortensen seemed a fine prospect, and in 1981 Derbyshire, having watched him with interest, invited him to return to England for a fortnight's trial. He had been recommended to the county by their former skipper Ian Buxton, and he impressed coach Phil Russell enough for him to suggest to the committee that the Dane be offered a contract.

With New Zealander John Wright and South African Peter Kirsten already registered, however, Derbyshire had their full quota of overseas players, and no offer could be made to Mortensen.

The Danish fast bowler returned to Derbyshire for another visit in 1982, and the following year, having given up his job as a tax inspector, he came to England to pursue his dream of becoming a first-class cricketer. Wright and Holding, who had now joined the Derbyshire staff, were engaged in the World Cup at the beginning of the year, and Wright, in fact, was available for only four matches because of his commitments to the New Zealand tourists who played a Test series in the second half of the summer, so that Mortensen was able to play at the beginning of the season.

In October 1982 Derbyshire's application that he should be

considered over and above their allocation of imported players was rejected on the grounds that he was not eligible for England. In June 1983 they again presented their case to the TCCB, who were advised that, on legal grounds, Mortensen's registration could not be opposed. Denmark, like Britain, is a member of the European Economic Community, and 'nationals of a member state must benefit in all other member states from the provisions of the Community concerning freedom of movement'. The matter was discussed by the registration committee, but they were powerless to stop a citizen of the EEC pursuing his trade in England under the provisions of the Treaty of Rome.

If one may be allowed a personal intrusion at this point, the present writer's elder son, resident in Copenhagen, is captain of KB, one of Denmark's oldest cricket clubs. In Denmark, there is a restriction on the number of foreign players that each club may field, and, on learning that the TCCB had been forced to yield on the question of Mortensen, KB approached the Danish Cricket Association on the status of Keith Lemmon. KB were neatly turned aside, the Danish Association ruling that whereas a man would go to England to seek a career in cricket, the same thing could not happen in Denmark!

From the first, Mortensen has been a great success with Derbyshire. No cricketer in the country is more enthusiastic, more eager to do well, nor more committed to a county to whom he feels the utmost gratitude. He took 84 wickets in all cricket in his first season with Derbyshire, and took part in a most memorable victory over Yorkshire, at Sheffield.

He had been welcomed at Derby and was soon nicknamed 'Stan' after the great England footballer of the 1950s, Stanley Mortensen. In the game at Sheffield, he took six for 57 and five for 62 as Derbyshire won by 22 runs, their first victory over Yorkshire for 26 years. He and Holding, with whom he has too infrequently been paired, represent one of the most hostile opening attacks in county cricket.

Following the example of Derbyshire, Hampshire enlisted the help of Dutch pace bowler Bakker, and Gloucestershire obtained the Zimbabwe all-rounder Kevin Curran.

Curran was born in what was then Rhodesia, and his father

played Currie Cup cricket for the former colony. Kevin Curran's grandparents were Irish, and he was able to travel on an Irish passport. This allowed Gloucestershire to register him under the same terms as Bakker and Mortensen were registered.

A right-arm medium-pace bowler and hard-hitting batsman, Curran was an immediate success in the West Country and was awarded his county cap in his first season, 1985. Even though injury prevented him from bowling for nearly all of the 1986 season, he held a regular place in Gloucestershire's championship side, scoring 1,353 runs, average 43.64. Gloucestershire were prepared to release him to play for Zimbabwe in the ICC Trophy, but such a move would have called into question his right to play for the county as a non-overseas player. In fact, by the time the tournament took place in June 1986, Curran had already been decreed ineligible for Zimbabwe by the Zimbabwe government.

He had returned to his own country at the end of 1985 and performed splendidly against the Young Australian side. In the fifth one-day international, he had wrecked the start of the Australian innings with three wickets in four balls and was obviously a better player for his season with Gloucestershire. However, in December 1985, the Zimbabwe government abolished dual citizenship and decreed that only Zimbabwe citizens, with Zimbabwe passports, would be allowed to represent the country at any sport. Reluctantly, Curran chose to retain his Irish passport, as to have surrendered it would have cost him his professional career with Gloucestershire.

Zimbabwe suffered another blow when Graeme Hick, the most exciting young batsman in England, learned that if he appeared for them in the ICC Trophy, he would violate his ten-year residential period of qualification making him ineligible for England. So he must wait patiently until 1994 before he appears in international cricket again. He will then be 28, and if he maintains the form he showed for Worcestershire in 1986, he will most likely be the best batsman in the world and certainly one of the most entertaining.

While the restriction on the number of overseas players was instigated with the approval of the counties, indeed the TCCB is the corporate voice of the seventeen counties, this has not pre-vented them from trying to utilise the existing regulations, and the loop-holes in them, to their advantage. There was a move to gain counties compensation for being allowed to play only one 'non-qualified-for-England' player, and the rule allowing a county to sign a replacement player on a one-year contract has been fully exploited.

Michael Holding played for Lancashire for part of one season when he was in the Lancashire League in 1981. In 1983 Derby-shire attempted to register him on a one-year contract, as John Wright was on international duty for the summer. The applica-tion was rejected, for, rightly, the TCCB refuses to condone a cricketer being used as a mercenary, moving from county to county for a single season, shoring up a gap caused by the absence of a Test player on tour with his country.

Derbyshire were only able to sign Holding if they offered him a long-term engagement, three years, which they did. He proved to be an invaluable acquisition, forming a splendid new-ball com-bination with Mortensen when the two were able to play together. Holding played only six matches in 1983, not at all in 1984 when he was with the West Indian side, twelve games in 1985 and fourteen first-class matches in 1986. The great problem arose in 1984 when, with Holding absent and Mortensen injured, Derbyshire included another West Indian in their side, fast bowler Devon Malcolm. Under the new regulations relating to overseas players, Derbyshire were allowed to field only one of their three importa-tions, Wright, Holding or Malcolm, at any one time. They had further complications at second eleven level where Cooper, a promising New Zealander introduced by Wright, had to be omit-ted after scoring a century in order to accommodate Malcolm.

In 1986 Derbyshire, anxious to use both Wright and Holding, for both batting and bowling were in need of a boost, proposed a reversion to the regulation allowing two non-qualified-for-Eng-land cricketers to play in each county side, but their move gained insufficient support. Nevertheless, by their action, they empha-sised the persistent conflict between 'the standards of English cricket' and the fortunes and finances of a county club.

Never was this conflict better illustrated than in 1981, when

England were faced with a crisis over the captaincy of the national side. The TCCB, anticipating that the problem could be a lasting one, issued a statement asking that all counties should appoint English-born captains so that the future of leadership at Test level would be assured. The response by the counties was for Lancashire, Kent and Worcestershire to appoint overseas-born captains, Clive Lloyd, Asif Iqbal and Glenn Turner respectively, and for Gloucestershire and Nottinghamshire to re-affirm their faith in the South Africans Mike Procter and Clive Rice.

Yet not all counties have had happy experiences with their overseas 'stars'. Glamorgan were to find that their importations were to be anything but a panacea for all ills. We have noted that they registered Majid Khan in 1968, and he and Bryan Davis helped them to win the championship the following year. In 1971 Davis decided to remain in the West Indies and concentrate on his business outside cricket. Majid was now recognised as being qualified through residence, so that Glamorgan were able to sign Roy Fredericks, the West Indian Test opener, an attacking left-handed batsman, on immediate registration. In this respect, he was luckier than Rupert Hill, who had been born in Jamaica and by 1972 had lived in England for four years. He had learned his cricket at school in Wales, but under the rules that existed at the time he was considered as 'overseas' because he had not lived in England for ten years. He ended by playing only one first-class match, against Cambridge University.

Fredericks began quite sensationally, hitting 145 and taking five wickets in his first match, against Nottinghamshire, at Trent Bridge. Tony Lewis immediately awarded him his county cap. Fredericks had a violent approach to the game, and there were some who believed that his attitude bordered on the irresponsible, but he hit 1,377 runs in 1971, topping the county averages, 1,199 in 1972, when he was second, and 415 in 1973, when he was third. He had been able to play only six matches in 1973 because he was assisting the West Indian tourists.

He expressed the view to interviewer Peter Walker that he would probably like to spend the rest of his playing career with Glamorgan, some ten years or so, but the county sacked him before the start of the 1974 season. At a time when Shepherd had retired, Majid Khan was with the Pakistan touring side and Tony Lewis was troubled by the injury which was to end his career that season, the dismissal of Fredericks came as a shock to the cricketing world. The committee who, it was alleged, reached the decision on a casting vote, stated that the county needed a bowler and that the time had come to give some of the younger batsmen greater opportunity. The only young player to be given extra opportunity, in effect, was Len Hill, who faded after one more season.

It was later asserted that Fredericks, who could be a great crowd-pleaser, did not try when playing for his adopted county. Certainly his overall performances were less than Glamorgan had the right to expect, and it is significant that Lewis, his county captain for two of his three seasons in the championship, makes no mention of him whatsoever in his book *Playing Days*, which covers the period with great sensitivity.

In Fredericks' place, Glamorgan registered Gregory Armstrong, a wild fast bowler from Barbados, who came with glowing reports of his prowess, but whose record for Glamorgan was miserable to say the least.

Meanwhile, since joining Glamorgan, Majid Khan had gone up to Cambridge where, as captain of the University, he had revitalised its cricket. In the winter of 1973, he was named as Pakistan's captain against England. The announcement came at the time that Intikhab Alam was leading Pakistan to victory over New Zealand. Not unnaturally, the appointment caused dissent among the Pakistan side, and Majid himself was replaced after three matches.

He succeeded Tony Lewis as Glamorgan's captain in 1973. It was not the best time to take over. It was the year that Shepherd retired and the last year of Roy Fredericks, who was to leave in such controversial fashion. Glamorgan had decided on a policy of rebuilding, and there was a growing unrest among county cricketers that although the game was being sponsored and publicised better, they were still on poor wages. Majid, a patrician of absolutely rigid Muslim principles, was hardly likely to be the ideal man to lead a struggling side in an atmosphere of disenchantment.

Eddie Barlow, another fine South African all-rounder. A medium-pace bowler and pugnacious batsman, he welded Derbyshire into a team. Backing up is Rohan Kanhai, Warwickshire's West Indian star.

Clive Lloyd, popular man, murderous batsman, who qualified for Lancashire through residence, after playing for Haslingden in the League. Both he and Engineer were soon accepted as Lancastrians.

Keith Boyce, a fine all-rounder who gave loyal service to Essex for eleven years. The county was very much his home, and the announcement in 1977 of his premature retirement through injury was an emotional moment for Essex supporters.

Clive Rice, sadly denied Test cricket, came to Notts via
Ramsbottom, and enjoyed the challenge of following Sobers.
Determined, intelligent, resourceful, there is no better captain in
world cricket. The batsman here is Ken McEwan of Essex, another
successful import from South Africa.

Zaheer Abbas, the elegant and prolific Pakistani batsman who, with
Sadiq Mohammad and Mike Procter, helped lift Gloucestershire
out of the doldrums.

Viv Richards, whose swaggering brilliance and glowing good humour won Somerset hearts when he signed for them in 1974. Three years later he was joined by his compatriot, the awesome giant Joel Garner (*above right*), and the pair did much to bring Somerset their first honours in 1979. The decision in 1986 not to re-engage them caused the biggest rumpus for years.

Bishen Bedi, of Northamptonshire, whose artistry, cunning and humour made him a popular acquisiton, but whose wages cost three young professionals their jobs.

Imran Khan, the glamorous and aristocratic Pakistani all-rounder, whose sudden departure to Sussex in 1976, after only one full season with Worcestershire, caused resentment.

New Zealand has provided county cricket with three outstanding performers. *Left:* Glenn Turner, one of the most successful of overseas players ever to appear in county cricket. In his first season at Worcester, 1968, he was known as 'the strokeless wonder', but five years later he reached a thousand runs by the end of May. *Right:* Richard Hadlee, whose hardwork and commitment set new standards at Trent Bridge. In 1984 he became the first player for seventeen years to complete the 'double', with Notts narrowly missing the championship. *Below:* Martin Crowe, rated so highly by Somerset for his batting and his example to younger players that they were prepared to let the idols Richards and Garner go . . . and to lose Botham.

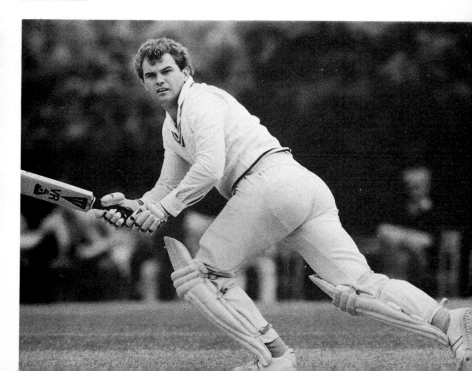

Faces of the future: Robin
Smith (*above left*), another
forceful South African
batsman who joined his
brother Chris at Hampshire
in 1982 and is qualified to play
for England. Graeme Hick, of
Worcestershire (*above*), who
played for Zimbabwe, the
country of his birth, but then
decided to spend ten years in
county cricket in order to
qualify for England.
Courtney Walsh (*left*), the
latest in a daunting line of
outstanding West Indian fast
bowlers, signed for
Gloucestershire in 1985 and
has twice bowled them close
to the championship.

He topped the Glamorgan averages in 1975, and they climbed from sixteenth to ninth in the county championship, but they were bottom of the John Player League at a time when the one-day game was rapidly becoming the most lucrative form of cricket for a county and its followers.

In 1976 the crisis point was reached. Tony Lewis records what happened: 'As criticism heaped up and the disloyalty both of the players and of the Glamorgan administration which once wooed him could be heard paraded on all home grounds, Majid returned to his introverted self of the sixties. On the field he thrust his hands deeply in his pockets, used his shirt collar as blinkers and carried on as best he could. His batting faltered, and the public which had crowned him in 1969 were now prepared to crucify. He was culpable, as I was before him, of lacking the appetite for one-day cricket. That is not to say that we did not try. Soldiering through the seventies without a world-class fast bowler was the current form of suicide, practised mainly by Glamorgan and Yorkshire.'

Majid Khan resigned the captaincy in July 1976, and a month later he walked out of the club for good. It was a sad and sordid end for a man of dignity and integrity who had been the hero of the county seven years earlier and now found himself vilified by those who had once appointed him and lauded him. As a distinguished importation, he had received the accolade for success; as an overseas captain, he was the scape-goat and paid the price of failure.

Glamorgan's next acquisition was Collis King, the West Indian all-rounder. He had played for Nelson in the Lancashire League with marked success, and, as a swashbuckling character, noted for his six-hitting, he was likely to be a tremendous attraction. In 1979, in the Prudential World Cup final, he was to play an innings in a stand with Viv Richards which was one of the most dynamic seen in recent times, but by then his Glamorgan days were over. His first season with the Welsh county, 1977, was a disappointment. He proved vulnerable with the bat and mundane with the ball. Perhaps Glamorgan expected too much of him, it was said.

He did help the county to reach the final of the Gillette Cup, but at Lord's he failed with the bat and dropped a vital catch at slip, a straightforward chance offered by Man-of-the-Match Radley when he was 2, and he was never quite forgiven for that. That first season was to be his last for Glamorgan. He went on his way to World Series Cricket, the rebel West Indian side in South Africa, league cricket, Natal and a few games for Worcestershire. He left only a memory of what might have been, but all too rarely was.

Peter Swart, a South African all-rounder, came in succession to King as Glamorgan's overseas signing. He played for two seasons, 1978 and 1979, taking 43 wickets and scoring 1,078 runs in his first season, and 17 wickets and 754 runs in his second. As this record suggests, Swart was an average county cricketer. He performed well in the Lancashire League, but he has never been among the top flight of South African cricketers. The same must apply to Warwickshire's Anton Ferreira. When the Midland county signed him he appeared to be little above good club standard. When Gooch hit a magnificent century against Warwickshire at Chelmsford in a Benson and Hedges Cup quarter-final in 1979, Ferreira conceded 72 runs in eleven overs. Gooch remarked afterwards that he could see no purpose in signing an overseas player unless he was going to help you to win something. Swart, like Ferreira, was never a good enough cricketer to tilt the balance of a match, nor to transform a mediocre county side into a trophy-winning one. As an overseas registration, he was an expensive luxury.

When Swart returned to league cricket Glamorgan were left with a vacancy for an overseas cricketer which was fortuitously filled by Javed Miandad. Javed had become available because Sussex, for whom he had played from 1976 to 1979, had also acquired the services of Kepler Wessels and preferred the rather ungainly run-accumulation of the left-handed South African in first-class matches to the more exciting and attractive batting of the Pakistani.

Javed has remained one of cricket's great enigmas. Off the field he can be a man of great charm; on the field, particularly in Test matches, he has been the centre of several unsavoury incidents – heated arguments with umpires and fielders and a fracas, bat raised, with Dennis Lillee among them. Before he had reached his 22nd birthday Javed had hit six Test centuries, and arguably only Don Bradman can match his sensational entry into Test cricket. Among contemporary batsmen no one has a better international record than Javed Miandad, yet neither Sussex nor Glamorgan have used his talents to the full.

When he joined Glamorgan he was quickly followed by Ezra Moseley, a fast bowler of a promise which had yet to find full expression in Barbados. Under the existing regulations, both were able to play in the county side in 1980, when Javed topped the county averages and scored 1,460 runs, and in 1981, when Javed hit 2,063 runs and again topped the averages.

The sufferer in 1980 was Rodney Ontong who had topped the batting averages the previous year with 1,157 runs, average 34.02, and taken 32 wickets. South African born, Ontong did not complete his ten-year residential period until 1981, when he was deemed as eligible for England, so that in 1980, with Javed and Moseley available, he played in only five matches. Cricket has not been too kind to Rodney Ontong. He became captain of the county in 1984, but resigned mid-way through 1986 when he lost his form.

Miandad had instilled greater punch into the Glamorgan side and given the batting 'a touch of class', but in 1982, as a member of the Pakistan touring side, he was able to play for the county for only half a season. *Wisden* insisted that he was 'missed as a brilliant, fast-scoring, match-winning batsman'.

More changes had taken place at Glamorgan before the beginning of the 1983 season. Mike Selvey had come from Middlesex to take over as captain, a job he was to find no easier than one of his imported predecessors, Robin Hobbs, and Moseley had departed to be replaced by the West Indian fast bowler Winston Davis. For the first part of the season Javed was absent with the Pakistan World Cup side, and he was also injured, but he now found himself back in the position in which he had been at Sussex. Under the existing regulations, he and Davis could not play in the same side, and Selvey felt that he needed a fast bowler more than he needed a batsman. Javed played in only four championship matches.

The debate between the respective merits of a fast bowler and a class batsman have not been restricted to Glamorgan alone, for, at various times, Lancashire have hinted that they were probably more in need of the bowling of Steve Jefferies or Patrick Patterson than they were of the batting of Clive Lloyd.

In July 1984 Selvey resigned the captaincy, but the season was equally dispiriting for Javed. As *Wisden* reported, 'Javed Miandad's season was a mixture of triumph and frustration. His brilliance as one of the world's top batsmen was undimmed, but his appearances were again limited by the restrictions on overseas players. Glamorgan had to recall Winston Davis, the West Indian fast bowler, in place of Miandad when Steve Barwick broke down in mid-August.' In eight matches, Javed scored 832 runs and was fourth in the national averages.

Winston Davis left the staff and Javed began the 1985 season with the possibility of playing in every match, but he suffered a recurrence of a 'mystery' back strain that kept him out for most of August, at the beginning of which month he had been the county's leading run-scorer. For the following season, 1986, Glamorgan re-engaged Ezra Moseley who, although playing league cricket, was to be available in mid-week so once again threatening to restrict Javed's appearances. As it transpired, the problem did not arise.

In April 1986 Pakistan competed in the Australasian Cup in Sharjah, an area of cricket insanely undervalued by the administrators in England and Australia. Pakistan reached the final where, before a capacity crowd, they met India, the reigning world champions. India made 245 for 7 in their fifty overs, and Pakistan were 242 for 9 when Javed shaped to face the last ball of the match, bowled by Chetan Sharma. He hit it out of the ground for six to give Pakistan victory and take his own score to 116. In Pakistan, work had come to a standstill as people crowded round radios to listen to the ball by ball commentary. Javed Miandad was a national hero. He was due to arrive in England and rejoin Glamorgan a week later. He went instead to Pakistan where he was feted in honour of his achievement. Glamorgan's efforts to contact him, when it was reported that he was ill and had domestic problems, proved futile. Javed was dismissed by the Club. He appealed against his dismissal, but the county stood firm.

There was no happy ending to the story. Moseley played in only six matches and took a poor eleven wickets. Dennis Hickey, a young fast bowler from Victoria in Glamorgan on an Esso Scholarship, played twelve games, but his seventeen championship wickets cost close to 60 runs each. For his part, Hickey, a delightful and enthusiastic young man, was elated by the opportunity that had surprisingly been given him and relished the experience. Glamorgan finished bottom of the championship table, 34 points adrift in spite of a victory in the last match of the season.

Mike Selvey, now a journalist for the *Guardian* and obviously still scarred by his short period as Glamorgan captain, wrote an article critical of Javed in which he insisted that the dismissal of the Pakistan Test player 'was merely the culmination of an association which was soured by the year and which was steadily undermining the fabric of the club.'

Selvey stated that Javed had always been difficult, consistently arriving in England late and contacting no one until he phoned from London Airport saying that he needed to be picked up. As Glamorgan captain, Selvey believed that his authority was undermined by Javed, and he said that other players lobbied him not to include Javed in the side, feeling that 'his contribution was often missing when it was needed most'. Javed's record does not support this view, but that is impossible to substantiate in any case, and what could be argued is that many of the county players were too content to leave it all to the overseas star, which has also been the case in some other counties.

Another part of Selvey's argument is that a good bowler would have brought more victories to Glamorgan than Javed did, but he tends to minimise Javed's contribution in an effort to prove his point. Moseley certainly is not the bowling equivalent of Javed the batsman, and although Selvey cites Holding, Marshall and Hadlee, he does not mention a bowler of comparable quality who was available for, or willing to play in, county cricket. Glamorgan signed a fine cricketer for 1987, Ravi Shastri, but he is a skilled batsman and a developing slow left-arm bowler, not a pace man.

Selvey entitled his article on Miandad's sacking, 'Few Tears in the Valley for Javed', but local correspondent Ron Jones, close to the events, cannot concur with this.

'What Selvey would not have quite understood, in spite of what may have been some very practical reasoning, is that Javed was and will be missed. The Welsh, you see, love a true sporting star. The little Pakistani master was the cricketing equivalent of a great rugby outside-half in their eyes – and to see him take the attack apart on a sunlit afternoon at Swansea was one of the sport's great joys. Difficult and unpredictable perhaps – but, boy, could he bat.'

More succinctly, a Glamorgan member in exile encountered at Maidstone in 1986 asserted, 'I wouldn't have renewed my membership if I'd known that they were going to get rid of him. He was a joy to watch.'

The circumstances in which Imran Khan left Worcestershire were rather different, and the resentment of the Worcestershire supporters is undiminished. Sussex, whose record with overseas players is rather bizarre, remain unforgiven.

Imran came to England with the Pakistan side of 1971. He was eighteen years old, raw and a little wild, if such a description can be applied to one whose mien has never fallen below the aristocratic. He was very inexperienced and took only twelve wickets on the tour and failed to score a fifty. He played in the first Test, did not take a wicket and was run out for 5. At the end of the tour he went to Worcestershire, played for the second eleven, scored a sparkling century and generally impressed.

He was found a place at Worcester Royal Grammar School where, in 1972, he excelled. He played for Worcestershire second eleven in the vacation. The following year, he was outstanding at Oxford and was allowed to assist Worcestershire in the second half of the summer when his pace bowling was a particular asset to the county.

In 1974 he was captain at Oxford, played all-round cricket of a very high standard and joined the Pakistan side for the second half of the summer a more mature and capable cricketer. Examinations dominated his life in his last year at University, but he still headed both the batting and bowling averages and performed well for Worcestershire at the season's end.

While in residence at Oxford, there was no hindrance to Imran assisting Worcestershire in the vacations, but in 1976, having come down, his status would be different, and he would have to be registered as an overseas player as he was no longer at an educational establishment.

In October 1975 Worcestershire requested that Imran be registered for the following season. They were told that this was not possible as the county already had its full quota of overseas cricketers in Turner, Holder and Parker. Parker, a New Zealander, had, like Turner, paid his fare to England, been engaged by Worcestershire and qualified in 1972. He was another who was to develop from a 'strokeless wonder' to a Test cricketer.

In January 1976 the registration committee's unanimous decision not to allow Imran to be registered was overturned by the Cricket Council, the game's highest authority, to whom Worcestershire had appealed. It was revealed that Imran, having been at boarding school in Worcester, had resided in the city since 1971. The registration committee had not been made aware of this fact, and they were not pleased with the Cricket Council's reversal of their decision.

So, in 1976, Imran played a full season for Worcestershire, scored 1,092 runs, took 65 wickets and was awarded his county cap. The county had a good season and reached the final of the Benson and Hedges Cup. At the end of the year, Imran informed Worcestershire that he did not wish to play for them any more. The county committee were angry and bewildered, and they were convinced that he had been offered large sums of money by another county. Allegations that he had been negotiating with Sussex and other counties while under contract to Worcestershire were rife, and the whole affair has never been fully explained to the satisfaction of all.

Imran's reasons for wanting to leave Worcestershire were set down in his 'ghosted' autobiography some years later. He stated that he found Worcester a boring place, that he missed Oxford, felt isolated and found little or no social life. The friends that he had made at school had all moved from the area, and he found himself travelling down to London at every opportunity. The Worcestershire secretary, Mike Vockins, suggested that he could live in London and travel to Worcester for his cricket, but he rejected this idea.

Imran accused Worcestershire of failing to provide him with adequate accommodation at the beginning of the 1976 season. It was generally believed that the county had paid for his education, finding him the place at Worcester Royal Grammar School and helping him through Oxford, but this Imran hotly denied. Nevertheless, none could deny that Worcestershire had made it possible for him to play in county cricket and that they had greatly helped in the development of his game.

For their part, Worcestershire felt aggrieved. They had engaged Imran when, although he had appeared in a Test match, he was a cricketer of unproven ability. They had welcomed him in England when few others took notice of him, and they had gone to a great deal of trouble to get him recognised as being qualified to play in county cricket, having provided him with the necessary residential qualification. In short, they had invested in Imran and received nothing for their investment.

In addition, D'Oliveira, Holder and, so it was thought, Gifford were all close to the end of their first-class careers, and Worcestershire's concern for Imran was that, at the age of 24, he very much represented their hopes for the next decade.

In effect, Worcestershire had been taken by surprise, and the wound that they suffered, whether in part self-inflicted or not, has never healed. Mike Vockins, in his charming short illustrated history of the county, makes little or no mention of Imran. Worcestershire opposed his move vehemently.

Imran contests that he was hurt by the slurs of disloyalty, that he had come to Worcestershire at the request of two people, Joe Lister and Wing Commander Shakespeare, both of whom had left, and that his salary had been cut by the new administration in 1972. The county still opposed his move, but at the beginning of 1977 he joined Sussex, being anxious to try his 'hardest for a dynamic captain like Tony Greig' and looking forward to playing on the Hove wicket. The TCCB were less impressed and, following an enquiry at Lord's, he was banned for the 1977 season for violation of contract and, by implication, of the ethics that are the fabric of the county game. On appeal, this ban was reduced and he was able to play for Sussex in the last month of the season.

The Professional Cricketers' Association deplored his transfer, and there was talk of some players refusing to play against him. It is interesting to note Imran's comments on one aspect of the controversy. 'Slurs were bandied about concerning disloyalty by overseas players, but I considered that merely a stick with which they could beat world-class cricketers who had done a great deal to keep some counties solvent and raise the standard of county cricket.' The man has always known his own worth.

Imran's case was not helped by the fact that he was also in dispute with the Pakistan Board of Control at the time of his move from Worcestershire, and that he was soon to join the Packer circus. He has continued to make his own terms, stipulating when and what type of cricket he should play, and presumably Sussex value him highly enough to allow him his way. Since he joined them, they have twice won the Gillette/NatWest Cup and took the John Player League in 1982 as well as finishing runners-up in the county championship in 1981. In the same period, Worcestershire have won nothing.

Imran is a handsome and highly talented man who has been greatly instrumental in raising the Pakistan Test side to its highest level of attainment. A fast bowler and an aggressively determined batsman, he is an all-rounder of the very highest quality, one good enough to represent any country as a batsman or a bowler. The evolution of modern cricket has made him one of the international jet-set group of cricketers, a Test-playing star who has not appeared in domestic cricket in Pakistan for several seasons even though he is captain of the national side. Injury and fatigue have necessitated that he should save himself for the big occasion.

At Worcester he remains unforgiven for his defection. They feel cheated, and when he bowled Sussex to victory over Worcestershire in the semi-final of the NatWest Trophy in 1986 the home supporters were quick to give vent to their long-felt frustration and anger.

The Imran affair was not the last to bring Worcestershire and Sussex into conflict, for there was also the strange case of Garth le Roux. The South African fast bowler played for Sussex against the New Zealanders in 1978, when he also appeared for the county second eleven. In 1979 they offered him a contract, but he was later approached by Worcestershire, whom he told that he had no commitment to any other county. At the beginning of July, he declined an offer that was made to him by Lancashire, and spoke again to Worcestershire. The county were of the opinion that he had agreed terms with them on 20 July, and two days later he was in contact with them again, saying, 'I'll be back to sign at 2.00.' At 1.30 he phoned Worcestershire to say that he was joining Sussex.

Investigations revealed that both counties had behaved properly, and there was no animosity between them over the business, but le Roux's registration was deferred until 1980.

What was now apparent from this incident was that although in 1968 some counties were guilty of signing overseas players on a somewhat haphazard and ill-planned basis, a decade later most counties knew exactly what they wanted, and usually it was a fast bowler. So important had the overseas cricketer become in terms of providing life-blood and personality to many sides that there was frequent exploitation of the one-year contract whereby one overseas cricketer could be imported to replace another who was on international duty. It is a system that does not meet with the approval of Test selectors, nor with the approval of some followers of the game.

Brian Johnston, the famous commentator, a man of great humour and humanity, resigned his Middlesex membership in protest at the importation of Jeff Thomson in 1981 when the fast bowler was not selected for the Australian tour of England. The previous year, Middlesex had used Vincent van de Bijl, and the big South African was immensely successful and popular. Both opened the bowling with Wayne Daniel, who has served Middlesex well and become more a part of the game in England than he has in the West Indies.

Some short-term signings have not been happy experiences; others have raised wider implications. In 1980, the TCCB approved a Somerset request for a full-season contract to Sunil Gavaskar on the understanding that he could never again be used as a short-term replacement for another county. In 1984 it was Martin Crowe who was used as Richards's replacement. Of this we shall say more later. Gavaskar began with a fine innings in a

Benson and Hedges Cup match against Kent, when he and Rose engaged in a record stand, and he did reasonably well thereafter. He arrived in Taunton with all his family, seemed mystified by the mechanics of life, such as the handbrake of a car, and, as Peter Roebuck pointed out, 'neither he nor his wife had the slightest notion of how to cook and wash without their retinue of servants'. He does not smoke, drink or swear and regards cricket as 'only a game', so that he was hardly the best-equipped cricketer to enjoy the county circuit. Yet, as Roebuck points out in his delightful essay on Gavaskar, the master batsman was most popular with players and spectators at Somerset and was responsible for something which could not be measured in the score-book; he set a standard in technique which young players attempted to imitate.

In 1984 Somerset attempted to re-engage Gavaskar as a part-season cover for Martin Crowe, who was himself a temporary replacement for Viv Richards. The request was rejected.

The same year that Gavaskar appeared for Somerset, Hampshire used Shaun Graf, an Australian fast-medium-pace bowler later to appear in international cricket, as a replacement for Malcolm Marshall. Graf proved to be a cricketer of limited talent, and a man unable to accept the disciplines of a county club, responding to his captain's request that he should come properly dressed to breakfast by appearing next morning in a dinner suit. When Hampshire were again without Marshall, in 1984, they turned to the West Indies and invited an unknown pace bowler, Milton Small, to join them for the season.

Small had played no first-class cricket when Hampshire approached him, but he made his debut for Barbados towards the end of January, took nineteen wickets for them during the season, won a place in the West Indies side against Australia and was selected for the party to come to England. He was never to play for Hampshire, who turned again to the West Indies for a replacement for their replacement. This time they engaged Elvis Reifer who, unlike his two brothers, had not played first-class cricket for Barbados. Elvis was finally to make his Shell Shield debut in 1986 when he appeared in one match.

Reifer, left-arm medium-pace, took 49 wickets for Hampshire at quite a high cost and the county finished in the bottom three of the championship, but he had fulfilled an ambition. At the end-of-season dinner, he said how grateful he was to have spent a season with Hampshire, for it had long been a dream of his to play for them. The Hampshire players remember him with much affection.

There was concern that the temporary registration measure could be abused, and Kent and Essex were two counties who were thwarted in their efforts. In 1977 Keith Boyce, the fine all-rounder who had been with Essex for eleven years, broke down and was never to play again. Essex attempted to register Richard Hadlee in July as a replacement for Boyce for the remainder of the season, but their request for special registration was rejected. The registration committee were only prepared to accept a long-term registration until the end of 1979. In fact, Hadlee was to join Nottinghamshire the following season.

Reasons for this have never been fully explained, but one, that comes from Richard's wife Karen, is that Essex, seemingly unaware of the time difference between England and New Zealand, phoned the Hadlees at three in the morning, New Zealand time. Karen suggested that her husband could play for whomsoever he chose, except a side that did not know when it was 3.00 am in New Zealand.

Kent were twice unlucky. In June 1981 they were denied when they attempted to sign Seeff, the South African batsman, for a part-season, and, in October 1982, their attempts to sign Abdul Qadir, the Pakistan leg-spinner, on a two-and-a-half-month contract were also over-ruled.

Two years later, Kent turned their attention to the Australian Terry Alderman. This fine pace bowler had bowled magnificently on Australia's tour of England in 1981, and he represented a splendid capture as a one-year replacement for Eldine Baptiste who was with the West Indian side. Kent have always felt that, although he is registered as an overseas player, Baptiste is essentially their product, for he had no first-class experience when they took him on, and they have shaped him as a cricketer.

Alderman proved an outstanding success in his first season with Kent. Dudley Moore, so close to Kent cricket, wrote of him: 'Alderman could not have given Kent better service. He took 76 championship wickets, bowled tirelessly and unselfishly, and his competitiveness and enthusiasm provided an invaluable inspiration for his colleagues in the pace- and seam-bowling department.'

The Australian had given Kent a taste of total commitment, and they were quick to recognise his value. They re-engaged him in 1986, even though they would be unable to play both him and Baptiste in the same side. He missed the first two matches and the last three, through injury, but the pattern emerged for Baptiste to play in the one-day games and Alderman in the championship matches. The Australian took 98 wickets, showing the qualities of commitment, stamina, determination and resolution of which every county dreams. Umpire David Shepherd was convinced that he was the best bowler in the country, and there were others who suggested that Kent would have won if he had played in the Benson and Hedges Cup Final at Lord's.

Kent were left with a West Indian Test all-rounder playing only in a forty-over slog on Sunday afternoons, and one wondered how long they could afford to pay the price of such a luxury.

Leicestershire, unable to play both Benjamin and Ferris, once seen as West Indies' next great fast bowler, and Derbyshire, for whom Holding and John Wright could not appear in the same match, faced a similar problem. By the end of 1985, the restriction on overseas players had brought to an end the career in England of one highly respected player.

In 1969, Surrey acquired the Pakistani all-rounder Intikhab Alam on immediate registration. A leg-spin bowler of high quality and a hard-hitting, exuberant batsman, Intikhab became a great favourite at The Oval. He captained Pakistan on the 1971 tour of England, and assisted Surrey in the second half of the season as they went on to win the title. Geoff Howarth, listed as a New Zealand right-handed batsman and off-break bowler, also played in one match that season, but it was stated that he had not been re-engaged. He had, in fact, been on the staff since 1969, and the announcement that he had not been re-engaged was premature, for he appeared four times in 1972. The following season, he had forged a regular place in the side and hit two centuries, including 159 against Kent at Maidstone. He was capped the next year when he was in the Surrey side which beat Leicestershire in the Benson and Hedges Cup Final. A few months later he made his Test debut for New Zealand.

In 1978 Roger Knight succeeded John Edrich as captain of Surrey, and Howarth could play only half a season because he was with the New Zealand side in England. He scored 74 in the Benson and Hedges Cup Final of 1979, when Surrey were beaten by Essex. Intikhab was also in the side, but Surrey now had a third overseas player, fast bowler Sylvester Clarke, who joined on immediate registration that season, but was unfit to play in the Benson and Hedges Final.

Neither Howarth nor Intikhab held a regular place in the Surrey side in 1980, but Clarke had emerged as one of the most devastating fast bowlers in the country. Surrey reached the final of the Gillette cup, but Howarth had no place in the side, and the following season he appeared in only eight championship matches. It was rumoured that he had domestic problems and that he was not in favour with Knight.

In 1982 he re-established himself. He scored over a thousand runs and played a sparkling innings in the NatWest Final. Surrey won easily, and Howarth took two stunning catches at slip. The next season saw him fully occupied in leading New Zealand in the World Cup and on their tour of England.

Howarth was recognised as one of the very finest of Test captains. A thinking man, he shaped the limited resources at his disposal into a team that was fired by self-belief, commitment to each other and an unquenchable desire to win. New Zealand cricket reached unprecedented heights. In 1980 they had a series victory over West Indies.

Roger Knight ended his reign as Surrey's captain at the end of the 1984 season, and it was apparent that Howarth should be his successor. Few counties have ever been able to boast of having one of the best Test captains in history as a ready replacement when their skipper retires. Howarth was named as Surrey captain for 1985, but events outside his control were to thwart him before the season began.

Sylvester Clarke had gone to South Africa with the 'rebel' West Indian side in 1982. His pace had made him an immense favourite, and he was offered a contract by Transvaal, who had dominated South African cricket for some years and who were to sweep all opposition aside with Clarke in the team. In 1984-85, however, he sustained a back injury, and when he returned to England it was immediately recognised that he would be unable to assist Surrey during the summer.

The Surrey reaction was swift. The philosophy of manager Mickey Stewart was that it is necessary for counties today to win a competition, and no county will win unless it has a fast bowler of quality. Anthony Gray had just enjoyed a record-breaking season for Trinidad. Surrey signed him on immediate registration. Howarth and Clarke were able to play alongside each other, for both had been registered before November 1978. Howarth and Gray could not play in the same team. Surrey felt that they needed a fast bowler more than they needed a captain-batsman. Gray took 79 championship wickets. Howarth played against Cambridge University and Zimbabwe. He left the county at the end of the season.

The ultimate limitation on the number of overseas-born cricketers eligible to play in a competitive county match was inevitable after the profligate years of the seventies, yet few could have fully realised the implications that restriction would bring. It became imperative that, limited to one overseas player, the counties were correct in the choice of the one man that they would engage.

In the quest for the cricketer who would give the side the balance that it needed, Warwickshire became entangled in some strange events in 1986. Alvin Kallicharran and Anton Ferreira were already registered for the county, and, having been engaged before November 1978, they were able to play in the same side. Warwickshire, however, suffered from a chronic shortage of bowling talent, especially pace bowling, and although Ferreira had developed considerably from the very average cricketer who had first appeared in 1979, he was not quick enough to trouble the best batsmen. Accordingly, the Warwickshire manager, David Brown, went to South Africa in search of fresh talent in the form of a pace bowler.

He returned with Brian McMillan, a young all-rounder, who

had fought his way into the Transvaal side and scored 419 runs in eight completed innings. He was also a useful medium-pace bowler. McMillan's potential was enormous and he won two Benson and Hedges Gold Awards in his first six weeks in England. One was for an innings of 51 against Leicestershire, the other for an innings of 76 against Derbyshire when he also took three for 22. This turned out to be his best bowling performance in any type of cricket throughout the season, which was hardly what Warwickshire were looking for from a strike bowler. He batted quite splendidly, scoring 999 first-class runs, average 58.76, but he took only seventeen first-class wickets at 47.52 runs each.

The matter was further complicated in that when McMillan played, Kallicharran could not, neither could Ferreira. For the first few weeks of the season, one of the finest batsmen in the world sat on the side-lines and watched a man engaged for his ability as a bowler score runs and take no wickets. Warwickshire attempted to have Kallicharran considered as 'English', for, indeed, he had long been settled in England, but he had played for West Indies as recently as 1981, and the appeal was rejected. When Kallicharran was brought into the side he hit four centuries in his first six matches. When he was injured in the game against Leicestershire McMillan returned and hit 134 against Yorkshire and 134 againsts Notts in successive matches. It was an irreconcilable problem. McMillan, the fast bowling hope, returned to South Africa one run short of his thousand. He finished fifth in the national averages, two places above Kallicharran who scored 1,005 runs. Warwickshire signed West Indian pace bowler Anthony Merrick for the 1987 season, and, like Scarlett O'Hara, decided to think about the problem tomorrow.

A wider problem asserted itself when the restriction on importations came into force. With their source of supply from overseas rationed, it was apparent that counties would be obliged to turn their attentions more and more to the English-born 'star' or potential 'star'. On the surface, this would appear to be a healthy state of affairs, but the TCCB recognised that it was a situation fraught with danger. With quality players in short supply, there could be a temptation to poach players or an increase in the movement of players between counties, neither of which would be in the best interests of the first-class game.

As early as 1984, the problem was discussed by the registration committee, and steps were taken to discourage such practices. Nevertheless, one factor still dominates the game and motivates the action that counties take, and that is the public's constant demand for success. Who or what, ultimately, will pay the price for that success at present remains unanswered.

PART 6
The Reward

In December 1960 Australia and West Indies played the famous tied Test at Brisbane. When the last eight-ball over of the match arrived Australia needed six runs to win, with three wickets standing. A single came from the first ball, and Richie Benaud was caught behind off Hall's second delivery. Australia failed to score off the third ball, but a bye was run off the fourth. Grout was dropped off the fifth ball and a run was stolen. This meant that three runs were needed for victory with three balls remaining. Meckiff struck Hall's fifth ball into the outfield, and the batsmen ran two to bring the scores level, but as they attempted the winning run, Grout was run out. Kline turned the seventh ball to square leg and he had Meckiff set off for what would have been the winning run, but Solomon swooped, picked up, threw and hit the wicket, seemingly all in one movement, and the match was tied.

Not unnaturally, the game roused tremendous excitement, and from that point on, the series was alight. Test cricket had been in a period of stagnation, but Australia and West Indies had revitalised it. The teams arrived for the final Test in Melbourne on level terms, and another thrilling encounter saw Australia win by two wickets. On the second day of the Melbourne Test, 90,800 people attended, and when the West Indians left Melbourne to return home they were given a ticker-tape send off such as is usually associated with the arrival of conquering heroes in New York. The sadness was that the West Indies were not scheduled to play in Australia again for another seven years. The Australian public demanded to see more of the cricketers from the Caribbean, and they had their way. The following season, Rohan Kanhai, Wes Hall and Gary Sobers returned to Australia to play Sheffield Shield cricket.

Kanhai was engaged as coach by Western Australia. At Adelaide, on the 1960-61 tour, he had become the first West Indian to score a century in each innings of a Test match, and he played eight matches in all for Western Australia in his one season with them, scoring 533 runs. He and Shepherd set up a state record for the third wicket with a stand of 223 against South Australia. In 1969-70, Kanhai returned to Australia to coach Tasmania.

In Brisbane, Wes Hall, the great fast bowler, was immensely popular, showing the same enthusiasm whether he was playing for the state side or in a grade match. He gave tremendous value in his two seasons and electrified cricket throughout the state.

Sobers, the world's greatest all-rounder, was the star capture, and he produced some memorable performances in his three seasons with South Australia. Eventually, he married an Australian girl and became a naturalised Australian.

He had caused great excitement in the 1960-61 Test series, hitting 132 in the tied Test, 168 in the third, and taking 5 for 120 in the fifth Test when he bowled unchanged for 41 eight-ball overs. Such performances led the Australian public to expect much of him, and he did not disappoint. In his first season, against New South Wales at Adelaide, he hit 251 in a spectacular second innings and then bowled spin to take six for 72 and win the match. The following season, he became the first South Australian player ever to score a thousand runs and take fifty wickets in a season. He equalled the record in his last season when he hit six centuries and South Australia won the Sheffield Shield. These were heady days, and they have stamped themselves indelibly on the memory of Australian cricket lovers.

The impact that Sobers, Hall and Kanhai made on the game in Australia should never be underestimated. The crowds thrilled to them, and in the following years, other cricketers were imported in an attempt to sustain the interest that had been aroused. Colin Milburn excited in Western Australia. Lance Gibbs entertained in South Australia, and Hampshire and Ibadulla did important coaching and playing work in Tasmania. The most significant and fruitful importation, however, was that of a veteran England slow left-arm bowler, Tony Lock, who joined Western Australia in 1962-63 and played for them until 1970-71.

Lock coached and played for four district clubs in the Perth area, captained the state side from 1963-64 onwards and helped lay the foundations to a coaching system which was to take Western Australia to a position of eminence in Australian cricket.

Western Australia had been admitted to the Sheffield Shield on a restricted basis after the Second World War. One of the conditions to their entry was that they should pay the expenses of state sides travelling to Perth for Shield games. This system was in operation for ten years. On a percentage basis they won the Sheffield Shield at the first attempt, but thereafter, their resources drained by their having to pay the fares of their opponents, they struggled to build a side of confidence and quality. That confidence was brought by Tony Lock, who effected a shift of the balance of power in Australian cricket.

Lock had tasted success and disappointment before he moved to Western Australia. That he was offered a contract by them in 1962-63 was because he had surprisingly been omitted from the England party that toured Australia that season. A tremendous fighter, he was just the man to rid Western Australia of their inferiority complex, and he instilled in them a will to win which culminated with him leading them to their first outright Sheffield Shield in 1967-68.

He had an infectious zest for the game which demanded a response from the spectators. He was a thinking, encouraging captain, and he led by the example of his splendidly controlled bowling, spirited batting and close-to-the-wicket fielding which has had no superior. In 74 matches for Western Australia, he took a record 316 wickets at 24.50 runs each, scored 1,467 runs, average 16.30, and held 85 catches. Australia took him to her heart, and he responded by becoming an Australian citizen.

The only other overseas player to have had an effect on an Australian state side comparable to that of Lock on Western Australia was Jack Simmons at Tasmania from 1972-73 to 1978-79. Simmons went to Australia as coach to the Northern Tasmanian Cricket Association. He did splendid work in Launceston, at school and club level, and began to have a profound influence on the organisation of the state side, which was trying to win a place in the Sheffield Shield competition.

Simmons had been hardened in the great days of Lancashire's limited-over triumphs, and his first memorable achievement for Tasmania was to lead them to their first ever victory in a Gillette Cup game when, against Victoria at Melbourne in 1974-75, he hit the last ball of the match for four.

In 1977-78, Tasmania were admitted to the Sheffield Shield on a trial basis, and Jack Simmons was named as captain. Tasmania acquitted themselves creditably, but the great achievement came in the Gillette Cup. Victories over South Australia and Victoria took Tasmania into the final against Western Australia in Perth, where they were beaten. The following season, they were again in the final, and with Simmons hitting 55 not out and taking four for 17, Tasmania reached the highest point in their cricketing history with victory over Western Australia. The impact on cricket in the island was tremendous, and Simmons coached boys on pavements and in the foyers of banks as he toured Northern Tasmania at the instigation of the Launceston Savings Bank. It was Simmons's last season for the state, and he has been followed by Davison, Hadlee, Williams, Butcher, Ellison, and the fiery West Indians Franklyn Stephenson and Winston Davis – all notable players, but Jack Simmons remains Tasmania's greatest hero.

If Simmons and Lock made mighty contributions as player/coaches, they were not alone in lifting morale and revitalising Australian domestic cricket at a time when such a boost was needed. Alvin Kallicharran, Majid Khan and Viv Richards each played a season for Queensland, who still search for their first Sheffield Shield championship. For South Australia, in 1982-83, Joel Garner took 55 wickets and thrilled the Adelaide crowds, and in 1985-86, Gladstone Small, a lesser personality, bowled with pace and panache. Within six months he had won a place in the England side. Imran Khan, in a period of recuperation, was a dynamic force in 1984-85 as New South Wales won both the Australian domestic competitions, the Sheffield Shield and the McDonald's Cup. The only consummate failure was Wayne Daniel, so reliable in English conditions, who took one wicket (T.V. Hohns) for 180 runs in his season with Western Australia.

The Australians have tended to import judiciously. Restricted (with the given exception of Tasmania) to one overseas player per state, they ask for – and generally get – a commitment beyond that of playing in the Sheffield Shield. Often cricketers, like Ken McEwan, who spent two years in Western Australia, have emphasised what they have received rather than what they have given. McEwan insisted that he learned what hard work was from those he coached in Perth, who would pound away and practise vigorously after a hard day at work. McEwan, whose career has spanned Essex, Western Province and Western Australia, is among a very select band who have played in a championship-winning side in three different countries.

His fellow South African, Kepler Wessels, went to Australia at the same time. Wessels had been something of a child prodigy. An outstanding sportsman at both rugby and tennis, he played three seasons in first-class cricket before leaving school. In 1976 he made over a thousand runs for Sussex second eleven, and played for Sussex against the West Indian tourists. The following season, he hit two centuries for Sussex before returning to South Africa to complete his national service. He played very little in 1978 and signed for Kerry Packer's World Series Cricket the following winter.

He had splendid seasons for Sussex in 1979 and 1980, but he had recognised the opportunity offered by Australia and settled there during the 1979-80 season when he first played for Queensland. A left-handed opening batsman and a rather ungainly accumulator of runs, Wessels was recognised as a tough, uncompromising competitor, and his form with Queensland improved year by year. In 1981-82, he became only the eighth player to reach a thousand runs in a Sheffield Shield season, and he repeated the feat the following season. He had become a naturalised Australian, and the Australian Cricket Board recognised that he would be eligible to play for Australia after September 1982. He scored 162 against England in his first Test.

Thereafter, Wessels batted mostly with success in Test cricket although he fared badly in the West Indies and had to return home early injured. He was moderately successful in Border's very weak side which toured England in 1985, but, on returning to Australia and playing in the first Test against New Zealand, he announced that he would not play for Australia again and that he would be returning to South Africa to take up a post at the University of Port Elizabeth. He had severed his links with the Australian Test side because he considered the length of contract and the financial terms offered him by the ACB to be derisory.

There was anger at Wessels's decision, and it was generally felt that he had exploited Australia and had used his Australian citizenship contemptuously. He had become Australian in order to play Test cricket; that having been achieved, he was ready to return to his native country. It was also hinted that he had played a major part in setting up the rebel tours made to South Africa by Kim Hughes and his team.

Wessels offered as the reason for his disenchantment with Australian Test cricket the constant press criticism that he was a South African and had no right to be in the Australian side. Warwick Hadfield, an Australian journalist who combined with Chris Harte on a book which investigated intelligently and deeply the events leading up to the rebel tour of South Africa, put forward the view that the ACB had been reluctant to offer Wessels more than a one-year contract despite his undeniable worth to the Test team because of the doubts as to his 'level of commitment to Australian cricket, in the past as well as the future'.

The defection of Wessels raised the whole question of overseas players in Australian cricket. There was anger, and the argument was again offered that the inclusion of overseas cricketers impeded the progress of young Australian players and retarded their attempts to move from grade to Shield cricket. This argument was countered by those who felt that the imports improved the standard of the Sheffield Shield at a time when standards were under threat. Wessels himself again reached a thousand runs in 1985-86, captained Queensland in the Sheffield Shield final in the absence of Border, and hit 166.

It was cited that Roland Butcher had averaged under 20 for Tasmania, that Younis and Daniel had been disasters and that Andy Roberts had broken down after two matches for New South Wales. But these arguments could be countered by reference to Gary Sobers, who had 'attracted spectators and provided excitement for three memorable seasons', to Tony Lock, whose 'imprint remained on the young players he had led, and the now highly competent West Australian team went on to dominate cricket in this country throughout the 1970's, and to Jack Simmons, from whom Tasmania demanded and received a great personal effort.

The quotations are from an article by Mark Browning in the *Australian Cricketer*, and his conclusion is the only sound answer to the argument, when he refers to 'the need for state authorities to be selective in the type of player they pursue ... they must clearly be of the highest class, keen to succeed and fit to perform'. Browning does not mention incentive, which certainly produced from one overseas player one of the most remarkable batting feats in Australian cricket since the war.

Barry Richards is one of the most brilliant batsmen in the history of the game, and we have seen no better player since Don Bradman retired. He played his first Test match, against Australia, at Cape Town in January 1970. It was the first of a four-match series in which South Africa outplayed Australia in every game, their lowest margin of victory being 170 runs. Richards scored 508 runs, average 72.57, in the four Tests. They were the last Test matches that South Africa were to play.

To a young player at the outset of what all believed would be an outstanding Test career, South Africa's excommunication came as a terrible blow. What would the history books of the game have said if Hobbs or Bradman had had his Test career ended after four successful matches? South Africa were due to play in Australia in 1971-72, and, in anticipation, Richards accepted an offer to play in South Australia in the 1970-71 season. The official tour was never to take place, but Barry Richards's one year in the Sheffield Shield was to set standards which have not been approached since.

There was criticism in South Africa that Richards had turned his back on the Currie Cup and Natal, but he received no business offer from his own country, and much of his career was to be closely linked to business.

The business offer came from the Prospect Club in Adelaide, who supplied Richards with accommodation. The Coca-Cola Company paid him a salary and supplied him a car. They also decided to sponsor him at a dollar a run and ten dollars a wicket (he was an occasional off-spinner). This situation later caused much adverse comment. Most of the criticism was aimed at what was called 'Richards's greed'. The batsman's answer was, 'I happen to be a professional cricketer, that's my training, that's my talent, and it's the only way at present that I can make myself a decent living. I'll not deny that the 'dollar a run' incentive I played for out in Australia made me a better player. Whereas before I'd been a sort of airy-fairy type of batsman with success coming pretty easily, that extra incentive made me a much more determined character and certainly more single-minded about making big scores.'

It is likely that the sponsorship would have been quickly forgotten had it not been for Richards's prolific scoring. He was dismissed cheaply by McKenzie in his first innings, against Western Australia in Adelaide, but hit 44 not out in the second as South Australia drew the match. His next match was against the England touring side led by Ray Illingworth. Richards hit 224 in six and a quarter hours, seemingly not even bothering to savage the attack, so easily did runs come to him. There were innings of 51 and 42 in the drawn games with Victoria, and then, on 20, 21, 22 and 23 November, South Australia went to Perth for the return match against Western Australia.

Western Australia were led by Tony Lock. Their opening attack was Lillee and McKenzie. Mann and Brayshaw completed the attack, with Inverarity's spin used occasionally. Ian Chappell won the toss, and Richards and Causby opened the South Australian innings. According to Richards, he missed the first ball of the match, a gentle out-swinger from Lillee. It was the last ball that passed his bat all day. He and Causby put on 109 for the first wicket, of which Causby scored 38. Richards and Ian Chappell, who was stumped for 129, then added 308 in 170 minutes. At the end of the five-and-a-half hour first day, South Australia were 513 for 3, Richards not out 325. It had taken a quarter of an hour's reconnaissance before he opened his score, but he reached his hundred in 125 minutes. His second hundred was scored in 83 minutes, and his third in 99. He batted for another 42 minutes on the second morning, adding another 31 runs before being l.b.w. to a full toss from Mann. He hit only one six, but 48 fours.

Following on his double century against the England side, the innings in Perth caused a sensation. His own recollection was, 'Somehow I managed to sustain for a complete day the sort of form that usually materialises only in short, glorious moments.' It was not the end of Richards's season of glory.

There was another century against MCC, successive hundreds against Queensland, New South Wales and Victoria, and then a broken finger in the last match, against New South Wales; but by then South Australia had won the Sheffield Shield. Richards had dominated the Australian season, 'often taking the limelight from the English team's tour'. As *Wisden* went on, 'Australians saw in the South African globe-trotting professional a complete batsman, combining grace and power with great technical skill.' He topped the Australian first-class batting averages with 1,538 runs, average 109.86. He had made a lot of money; and he had given a lot of pleasure.

He insists that playing Sheffield Shield cricket came as a bonus, that he went to Adelaide to play for the Prospect Club and to coach and undertake promotional work for the sponsors, Coca-Cola. He, Greg Chappell and athlete Kerry O'Brien were kitted out in special uniforms and did the circuit of lunch and dinner speaking engagements. He had not taken it for granted that he would play state cricket and considered his Shield appearances as the 'biggest perk of all'. 'There had been no guarantee when I signed with Prospect; simply that they would put my name forward for selection. They took a chance on me at the start, because within Australian cricket certain objections had been raised against playing foreigners. I like to think that I returned the favour.'

There are those in Australia who feel with gratification that at least they caught a glimpse of him once.

There are many who have never forgiven Barry Richards for that season in Australia, or rather have not forgiven him for publicising the money he received for his efforts. Like Anthony Trollope, who revealed in his autobiography the amounts that he had been paid for each of his novels, Richards had, in many people's eyes, debased his art by mentioning money. The *Wisden* comment on his prowess was tinged with the epithets 'globe-trotting professional', and Alan Gibson speaks of him as a cricketing Wallenstein. Wallenstein, the Austrian general in the Thirty Years War, was removed from his command when the Emperor suspected that he was about to abandon the Imperial cause, and he was later murdered by some of his officers who believed that he was going to defect to the Swedes. Gibson makes the comparison because it was said of Wallenstein that 'no man could divine his motives, and he had no country of his own'. In one respect the comparison is unfair to Richards, for in the international cricketing sense, he had his country taken away from him.

He was blessed with ability at the game of cricket not given to ordinary mortals, and yet his chance to display his talent at the highest level was taken away from him after two months, four matches. On top of this, as he admitted in an interview with Peter Walker, 'I've a dread of insecurity – my father had a tough time when I was in my early teens – redundancy and all that goes with it – and the spectre of poverty and the avoidance of it used to haunt me continually.'

He was captain of the South African Schools' side that toured England in 1963, made his first-class debut for Natal in 1964-65, and the following summer came to England, with Mike Procter, and played for Gloucestershire second eleven. Richards played for the county side against the South African tourists and scored 59. Gloucestershire wanted to keep him and asked him to qualify, but he declined. 'To qualify we would have had to spend the full winter in England, which would prevent any Currie Cup cricket. Though flattered by the attention, I had no doubts. The ladders I wanted to climb belonged in Natal.' Sadly, of course, the top rung of the ladder was to be removed a few years later.

Natal were the dominant force in South African cricket and won the Currie Cup every season from 1959-60 to 1967-68. In that final season, Richards scored four centuries in six matches. It was during that season that the authorities in England introduced the immediate registration rule. Gloucestershire signed Procter. Sussex wrote to Richards; Hampshire phoned him. Hampshire offered him a three-year contract at £1,300 for his first season. The Sussex offer was little more than half of that.

He found his reception in England far from friendly. Some

senior Hampshire players were envious of the money he was being paid, and, in an interview, he said that he aimed at scoring two thousand runs. In fact, he scored 2,395 runs in a wet summer, was second to Boycott in the national averages and Hampshire climbed from twelfth to fourth in the championship table.

The following season, he was hampered by injuries, but he still scored 1,440 runs, average 57.60, and was fourth in the national averages. Hampshire were fifth in the championship and second in the newly formed John Player League.

The county disappointed in 1970, when Richards played for the Rest of the World side against England. The hastily arranged series was scant compensation to him, Procter, Pollock and Barlow for the cancellation of the tour by the South African side for which they had all been selected. There was unrest in Hampshire at Roy Marshall's captaincy, and the fine West Indian stood down at the end of the season after glorious service. Gordon Greenidge appeared in the side for the first time. Marshall played for two more seasons, but this was a time of great change at Hampshire with players being released and moving to other counties. Richards stayed with Hampshire until 1978, and during that time, and very much because of him, Hampshire won the county championship, in 1973, and the John Player League, in 1975 and 1978.

Hampshire had gathered together a side from differing backgrounds and countries. The opening pair of Richards and Greenidge was the most dynamic in England, and Greenidge was soon to be joined by another West Indian, fast bowler Andy Roberts. Roberts replaced New Zealander David O'Sullivan, a slow left-arm bowler, who was 'reluctantly released' at the end of the championship season. *Wisden* reported that, 'Under the regulation allowing a county only two overseas players, Hampshire, with Richards one, were forced to choose between O'Sullivan and Roberts, a 22-year old genuinely fast bowler from Antigua. They wanted to keep both, but were forced to choose and the vote went to Roberts, who began his qualification period at the start of the season. No doubt that there are now three one-day competitions influenced Hampshire's decision.' Another influential factor was that O'Sullivan's action was suspect, but at least he can claim that he played in a championship-winning side.

In his eleven seasons with Hampshire, Barry Richards scored 15,607 runs, average 50.50, and played in 204 first-class matches; yet, it has been said, his heart was never in the three-day game. Certainly some of his most excitingly beautiful innings were played in limited-over cricket.

He scored over a thousand runs for the county in every season except the last two, by which time he had become totally disillusioned. Like Andy Roberts, he walked out half-way through the 1978 season and joined the Packer organisation. The excommunication of South Africa from Test cricket doomed him to seasons with Hampshire without the promise of anything different. He wrote, 'Though it has been a voluntary sentence, I have felt like a prisoner within the system.'

Greenidge, who is the first to pay tribute to Richards for the help and advice that he was given when he came into county cricket, says that Richards was visibly bored by 1977. The man had so much talent, and it had not been properly tested since he was 24 years old. At the age of 32, he could only look back on what might have been. He began to despair of the county game where 'the routine is interminable: every match is a carbon copy of the last'. Towards the end, he would throw his wicket away, for the scoring of runs no longer held any delight for him.

His criticism of cricket in England, his apparent contempt for the average county cricketer who enjoyed this mode of life, and the manner of his going won him few friends, but Greenidge states that Richards was seen by those present to be crying when he wrote out his letter of resignation.

He has perhaps suffered more than most because he has so often been the spokesman on money matters, negotiating for a larger income with Hampshire and with other organisations, but, as his countryman Ken McEwan pointed out, 'Barry was the brave fore-runner in financial negotiations. He made a great deal possible for others who have followed him.' McEwan also believes that he has never seen a better batsman than Barry Richards.

Alan Gibson is less kind. 'He was one of those whose career would have taken a different course, had it not been for the cricketing breach with South Africa. The new career which he adopted – he was the first of the really high-class *caballeros* to roam the world – brought him much more money than an ordinary Test career would have done. Whether he is better pleased with the outcome is hard to say. Many men who feel deeply take care to conceal their feelings; others appear unemotional because they have no deep emotions.'

For Richards, emotions are private. He was one who walked off at Newlands, Cape Town, in 1971, in protest against racial discrimination in team selection in the Republic, but he resents questions on his beliefs, wishing to talk to the press only about cricket and cricketers, the things about which he feels informed.

The argument over Richards will never be resolved. For those who saw him, he remains the finest batsman to have played since the war; and were it not for Hampshire, and the Immediate Registration rule of 1968, he might never have been seen in first-class cricket in England.

At the same time that Richards left Hampshire, Andy Roberts also walked out. One of the best half-dozen fast bowlers to have played cricket in the last forty years, Roberts served Hampshire splendidly and could be devastating upon occasions. He was a great source of entertainment and played a decisive role in the county winning the John Player League in 1975. He was asked to bowl a tremendous amount, and it was Gilliat's demands on him in this respect that led to his walk-out half-way through the 1978 season. He was accused of being a subversive influence, a rumour that was fuelled by his unsmiling nature, and he was certainly one who lived mostly in his own world, but he worked hard for Hampshire until he felt that he had had enough and been overworked.

He returned to play for Leicestershire on a limited basis from 1981 to 1984. A more mature man by this time, he gave them some wise counsel and brought them Ferris.

Throughout it all, Greenidge has continued to lash the ball to all parts of the ground, at one time holding the individual record for the highest score in all three limited-over competitions. For a batsman of such aggression, he is remarkably consistent, and a thrill of expectation shivers through the crowd whenever he goes out to bat. His career with Hampshire has not been without its crises, the latest of which came at Lord's, in August 1986. Hampshire were challenging well for the title and, in a rain-marred match, they were left to make 224 to win. They had reached 129 for 3, with Greenidge on 70, when he decided of his own accord that it was no longer worth pursuing the runs and walked off the field.

The incident caused some disturbance in the Hampshire camp, and Greenidge was taken to task. His response was to finish the season with successive innings of 222, 103, 180 not out, 126 and 30, and to play a dominant part in Hampshire's winning of the John Player League. Perhaps, like Richards, he is one who needs a renewed challenge from time to time.

The John Player League title in 1986 was Hampshire's first trophy since the departure of Richards and Roberts, and it was brought about by a good team effort, and the inspiration of Greenidge and Marshall. Marshall's commitment to the Hampshire cause has been total, and his worth to the side can be measured in statistics.

He joined Hampshire in 1979, when he was not yet established in the West Indies Test team, but shortly to be recognised as the fastest bowler in the world. He took 134 wickets in 1982, and Hampshire were third in the table, as they were the following season when, his appearances limited by the World Cup, he took 80 wickets. In 1984 he was with the West Indian side. Hampshire finished fifteenth. With Marshall back again, and taking 95 wickets, the county climbed to second place in 1985.

On top of this, they challenged strongly in all limited-over competitions, being semi-finalists in the NatWest Trophy in 1983 and 1985. With Marshall and Greenidge, Hampshire were one of the most forceful and exciting sides in the country; without them, they were just another county.

While it is easy to say that Marshall has kept a young English bowler out of the side, the paucity of bowling talent that was available to the county when he was on Test duty was apparent to all, and Parks and Tremlett would argue that they have become better cricketers through playing with him.

The morale-boosting effect that the advent of a top class player can have on a side is incalculable, although Gloucestershire supporters would say that is not the case: just look at their county pre-Procter and at what happened after his arrival in 1968. He was the fast bowler that Gloucestershire had been searching for throughout their history, but he was something more than that.

He was vice-captain of the South African Schools' side that came to England in 1963, and from that point, his career ran parallel to that of Barry Richards. When the Immediate Registration rule came into operation Gloucestershire attempted to sign Gary Sobers. They had a Centenary Year approaching, their membership was flagging dreadfully, and he was the greatest attraction in cricket. Sobers went to Notts, and Gloucestershire had to choose between Richards and Procter. They believed that Richards was already attracted to Hampshire, and so they settled for Procter.

By 1972, Gloucestershire had added Zaheer Abbas and Sadiq Mohammad on residential qualification, and the two Pakistanis, in conjunction with Procter, helped to make Gloucestershire one of the most attractive sides in the country. The county finished second in the championship in 1969, and they began to blaze a glorious trail through the one-day knock-out competitions.

The team was party to some epic struggles. In 1971, they reached the semi-final of the Gillette Cup and met Lancashire at Old Trafford. Procter led the assault on the home side's bowling. He hit a six and nine fours in an innings of 65. In full cry, he was a wonderful sight, a magnificent blend of invincible power and human vulnerability. He was out when Engineer caught him marvellously off Peter Lever's bowling. Gloucestershire had reached 229 for 6 in their 60 overs. Lancashire began slowly in reply, but their foundation was solid and the end, when it came, was dramatic. In near darkness, Tony Brown was reluctant to recall his pace men, Procter and Davey, and David Hughes, in a memorable innings, which included 24 in one over by Mortimore, hit off the runs. The match did not end until 8.56 pm, television coverage having been extended to include the finish of a game which has come to be regarded as a 'classic'.

Two years later, Gloucestershire reached their first Lord's final. This time they had Sadiq and Zaheer in the side. Both scored well in the first-round victory over Glamorgan. In the second round, they recovered from 24 for 5 to beat Surrey, and Essex were beaten in a thrilling quarter-final at Chelmsford. This brought them to Worcester for the semi-final. Choosing to bat first, Gloucestershire were 29 for 2 when Procter came in. He was majestic. There was always a languidness in his powerful elegance, and it made him one of the most exciting of batsmen. He made 101, and Gloucestershire finished with 243 for 8. It didn't seem enough when Worcestershire reached 188 for 3. Glenn Turner had hit 109 when Procter returned for his last three overs and took three wickets for 31, including that of Turner.

Gloucestershire had won nothing since the days of W.G. Grace, and the West Country responded with an enthusiasm that few in the area could remember. They came from the West in their droves and descended upon Lord's in high spirits. These spirits were soon dampened. Roger Knight fell to Snow; Sadiq and Zaheer fell to Michael Buss; 22 for 3 in ten overs. But Procter was there, head up, frightened of no one. He saw off Snow and hit Michael Buss for two sixes. He played an innings of passion and power, and he was out, caught at deep fine leg, for 94, attempting to hit the six that would have given him his century. Tony Brown followed Procter's innings with a splendid 77, hitting 46 of the 68 runs scored in the last eight overs, and Gloucestershire reached 248 for 8.

Sussex were appearing in their fifth Lord's final, but they could never quite come to terms with the task that faced them. A solid foundation was laid, but when the final burst was needed they were again confronted by Procter, who finished with two for 27 as Gloucestershire won by 40 runs.

When Gloucestershire next returned to Lord's for a final in 1977, Mike Procter had taken over as captain from Tony Brown. Kent, a most experienced and successful one-day side, were well beaten, and it needed no great Procter magic to bring about the win, although there was a delightful 70 from Zaheer. The deciding game in that Benson and Hedges Cup success had been in the semi-final at Southampton on 22 August.

Sadiq and Andy Stovold put on 109 for Gloucestershire's first wicket, but the rest of the side failed to build on this, and

Gloucestershire were all out for 180 in the last over of their allocation. The task seemed easy for Hampshire, but in a spectacular spell of fast bowling Procter tore the heart out of the home side's innings. Bowling round the wicket, he bowled Greenidge with the fifth ball of his third over, and with the first three balls of his next over he had Richards and Jesty l.b.w. and bowled Rice. He returned to dismiss Taylor and Stephenson after Hampshire had effected a recovery, and Gloucestershire won by 7 runs. No man was more able to turn the course of a match by his own supreme effort.

Gloucestershire came within five points of winning the championship that year, 1977, and Procter, inspiring by his leadership, took 109 wickets and scored 857 runs. There have been aesthetically more pleasing actions than Mike Procter bowling, but none which has had quite his dramatic quality. The momentum of the long run increased smoothly, and then he exploded into a delivery stride that was an awesome whirling action. He projected his weight forward, which gave the impression that he was bowling off the wrong foot. He put immense strain on himself, and he went back to South Africa at the end of his first season in county cricket with his knee in plaster, but he never spared himself. If he had a failing, it was that he never spared other people either.

John Childs, like all who played with him, remembers Procter with affection and deep respect, but, 'The only trouble with Prockie was that he was so good he thought everybody else should be the same. He was always scoring runs, taking wickets or making catches, and if you weren't doing the same, he thought you weren't trying.'

Cricket all over England thrilled to him, and in Gloucestershire they loved him, for he became one of them. He identified himself so wholeheartedly with the county that he became part of the scene. One could see him walk round the ground at Bristol with his baby in his arms, chatting to spectators here and there. It was no ostentatious display by some superstar; it was merely 'our Mike' strolling among his friends. He gave so much, but he learned much too.

'Not until I played professional cricket in England did I realise that the black man wasn't inferior to me. I was brought up in a typically middle-class South African environment and you just didn't question the laws of the land. In my naïveté, I assumed apartheid was correct because it was there. When I first came to England, I couldn't get over the sight of white men sweeping the streets and doing other menial tasks. I'd always assumed that was the lot of the black man ... But my eyes were opened when I started playing against and with decent civilised men like Clive Lloyd, Basil D'Oliveira, Gary Sobers and John Shepherd. They opened my eyes about racial discrimination and made me realise how blinkered my attitude had been.'

In Alan Gibson's words: 'Cricket has been a civilising influence upon Procter, but so has Procter been a civilising influence upon cricket.'

He embraced World Series Cricket with enthusiasm, because it offered him a belated opportunity to test his skills at international level, but it did not detract from his commitment to Gloucestershire. In September 1980 the TCCB registration committee, having examined Procter's movements and habitat since 1965, came to the conclusion that, as he had played in England since 1968 and had played the last of his seven Test matches for South Africa as long ago as 1970, he should be considered as being eligible for England. The reaction of Robin Marlar in *The Sunday Times* was immediate: he advocated that Procter should be sent as vice-captain of the England side that was due to go to the West Indies under the leadership of Botham.

This did not happen, and in any case, the TCCB's decision, which also concerned Brian Davison, was one of convenience for the counties rather than a pointer to England selection.

Procter disturbed the ruling a year later when he played for South Africa against Gooch's South African Breweries' England XI, but he was then 35, and the Test career of one of the greatest all-rounders the world has seen had been restricted to seven matches between the ages of 21 and 24.

The knees which had taken such a terrible battering over the years gave more trouble and, in 1981, he had to return home to South Africa for major surgery. His time with Gloucestershire was over, and he limped out of their history. Grahame Parker, the county's historian, recalls the passing of 'the greatest match winner in the history of the club'. 'His tempestuous career in every dimension of the game was over. His figures for Gloucestershire are 14,441 runs, 833 wickets and 185 catches, but cold statistics can never relate to the excitement of watching him bat and bowl. Never again would we see that long run gathering momentum to the mid air explosive blast at the wicket. Cricket is the poorer with his passing.'

Even as this is written, there is a rumour that Procter would like to come out of retirement and have a crack at Hughes's Australian side. He is close to 41, and he would probably have to concentrate on the off-breaks which he bowled so effectively for Gloucestershire on occasions, but one would not bet against him scoring the fastest century of the season, again.

The grace of Zaheer and the watchful application of Sadiq gave Gloucestershire cricket in the seventies a dimension of elegance and promise. Arguably, three overseas players of such stature as Procter, Zaheer and Sadiq were an extravagance, but between them they lifted Gloucestershire out of the doldrums and put them on the road to financial recovery which has been reflected in ground improvements and better utilisation of resources at Bristol.

When they departed, Gloucestershire cricket was again threatened with a vacuum, and the brief appearances of fast bowler Franklyn Stephenson failed to fill the void. Then, in 1985, the young West Indian pace man, Courtney Walsh, began to stir the emotions of the West. In 1986, he swept all before him as he took 118 wickets and brought Gloucestershire very close to winning the county championship.

The present writer approached him during the season, and he voiced his commitment to the county, saying that he had been delighted to 'give county cricket a try'. His team-mates said something more significant when they learned that the project in hand was a book about overseas players. 'He's not overseas. He's one of us.' That was Procter's strength. It could well turn out to be Walsh's.

At the time that Procter was signed by Gloucestershire, Essex registered Lee Irvine, another South African and a wonderfully free scoring left-handed opening batsman. Like Richards, he was to play impressively in four Test matches in 1970. He set the mould for Essex overseas signings in that he was little known, and therefore, one suspects, came cheaply to a county who had to observe economic restrictions at the time. He entertained and was well liked, but his passage was brief, as was that of his successor, the Australian opening batsman Bruce Francis.

Like Irvine, Francis was an unknown when he joined Essex and, like Irvine, he went on to play Test cricket. He was a tremendous hitter of the ball, but never gave the sense of a permanent attachment to the county, or indeed to cricket.

Essex already had one overseas player on the staff before Irvine joined them. Keith Boyce, a West Indian all-rounder, had begun a residential qualification in April 1965. Ten years later, he was to be recognised as a bona fide permanent resident.

Boyce came to Essex by way of Trevor Bailey, who was the Essex captain at the time. Bailey was playing for the Rothmans Cavaliers in the Caribbean and came up against Boyce when Barbados turned out a weakened and inexperienced side against the tourists. 'He proceeded to bowl fast (if not by some West Indian standards, at least by ours), hit the ball with exceptional power, field beautifully, and throw with sufficient velocity to have a flat trajectory from boundary to stumps. I have always believed that if you intend to bring an overseas player into county cricket, unless he is an established international star he should be a spectacular performer who will automatically excite spectators. Consequently, before the end of the game I had signed on Keith Boyce for Essex and informed my club of my decision.'

This was a stroke of genius on Bailey's part. Boyce was adopted at Essex, and he always considered himself a man of Essex. When, in 1977, at Southchurch Park, Southend, it was announced to the public that, because of a serious knee injury, he would never play for Essex again, it was one of the most emotional occasions one can remember witnessing at a first-class match. The measure of the man was that he begged Essex to keep his registration in the hope that he might get better.

From the very start, Boyce was a spectacular success. He bowled fast and he loved hitting sixes. He wound himself into a ball at the crease and uncoiled violently like a spring. There was supple movement in all he did, and at a time when one-day cricket was coming into vogue, he was ideally suited to this type of game. He became the first man to score a thousand runs and take a hundred wickets in limited-over cricket, and he went on to represent West Indies with considerable success.

To the end of his career, even after he had gained fame, and extra pace, at Test level, Boyce insisted that it was Essex who had given him the chance to become a cricketer and had shaped his progress. He loved the county, and Tom Pearce, who has been captain, chairman and president of the club, says that whenever Essex failed, Boyce took the blame upon himself, saying that he alone was responsible for the lack of success. He was a cricketer for whom the word dynamic is an inadequate description.

In his last seasons with the county, dogged by injury, he struggled, and he was never to be part of the great success that came in 1979 and the years that followed. Essex attempted to sign Hadlee as a replacement, but that was thwarted, and they returned to their policy of engaging little known cricketers who, under their care, developed into Test players. Norbert Phillip, who joined the club in 1978 and left in 1985, tended to remain a quiet, shadowy figure, known by few, but he provided the county with a dimension that won them honours for the first time in their history. He was no Boyce, particularly in the field, but he could hit a ball and he bowled quickly, and that was the missing part of the jigsaw puzzle that Essex had needed to turn them into champions.

Another player who left the club in 1985 was Ken McEwan, who had first played for the county in 1974. To sign a shy, young batsman from South Africa who had had very limited first-class experience, who had, in effect, been rejected by Sussex after playing for their second eleven and whose sole contact with Essex had been in a friendly match in Scotland, showed a perspicacity on the part of Insole and the Essex management which has been the crucial factor in their success. There were those who believed that engaging McEwan as an overseas cricketer when the quota of importations was being limited was a madness. They were to be proved very wrong.

McEwan captained the South African Schools' side in 1970. A protégé of Tony Greig's, he was seen in some quarters as his country's next Barry Richards or Graeme Pollock. He was to have led a schools' side against an Australian side, but the tour never took place. South Africa were banned from Test cricket. McEwan's one ambition had always been to become a professional cricketer, and England was the only country in which that ambition could be fulfilled.

Always nervous, basically shy, never completely believing in his own outstanding ability, he batted with an ease, audacity and eloquent grace that made him one of the most appealing sights in county cricket since the war. He had the full range of shots, and he wanted to use them. He never allowed himself to be dominated. He was always on the attack.

He scored 18,088 runs for Essex in first-class matches, with 52 centuries. There were another 5,531 runs in the John Player League, 1,925 in the Benson and Hedges Cup and 842 in the NatWest Trophy. He was a joy to watch, and, in his eleven years with Essex, it is doubtful if anybody ever looked upon him as an overseas player, for although he played for a time in Australia and, of course, in South Africa, his major achievements and ninety per cent of his cricket were with Essex.

Gooch believed him to be unique in that the major importations were bowlers, for it was bowlers that counties needed to help them win trophies, yet McEwan batted Essex to success. He was a member of an Essex side that won all four major competitions, and Lord's had its last gracious sight of him in the NatWest Final of 1985. It came as a shock when he announced that he would not be returning, but his reasons were understandable. 'I've been driving up and down the motorways of England for eleven years, and no prospect of Test cricket at the end of it.' He gained some consolation in playing against the rebel West Indian and Australian sides, for he had at last put on the green and gold which had been the childhood dream.

If McEwan's retirement came as a shock, the announcement that Allan Border would be his replacement came as a greater shock. This was a break with tradition in that Essex were now importing a ready-made star, something that they had assiduously avoided doing in the past. Manager Peter Edwards refuted the suggestion that the signing of Border was a publicity act. He stated that Border was engaged because Essex needed a batsman to replace McEwan and to guide their younger players. The Australian captain, however brief his stay, did what he was asked, and what was expected of him.

He scored more runs than any one else in the county side. He gave invaluable help to youngsters like Paul Prichard, and they were better for having known him. He conducted himself with dignity, courtesy and never failed to respond to the public relations demands made upon his time by those who were employing him and sponsoring him.

He left Essex at the beginning of August 1986, but, even without an overseas player in the side for the last month of the season, the county won vital games at Taunton and Folkestone and took important points against Gloucestershire, Surrey and Nottinghamshire to win the championship. Their triumph was the result of a calculated policy which had made their importations servants of the club, integral parts of a team, rather than masters or messiahs from whom salvation was expected.

The search for salvation is not always successful, as Derbyshire discovered. In 1970, they engaged Chris Wilkins, described by *Wisden* as 'the most successful newcomer in the history of Derbyshire cricket'. Wilkins, a powerful batsman and occasional medium-pace bowler, helped the county to third place in the John Player League in his first season, and stayed with them for three years, scoring 4,060 runs and taking 47 wickets. He was a good player, but perhaps not quite good enough to occupy part of an overseas quota. A South African, he was not in the Richards, Procter or McEwan class.

Surprisingly, he was replaced by Venkataraghavan, the Indian off-break bowler. The mid-seventies were the period when the Indian spinners were at their peak, and Bedi, Prassana, Venkataraghavan and Chandrasekhar were a dominant force in world cricket, yet whether they were of the temperament or style to suit county cricket is doubtful. In India, and in Test cricket, spin bowling is an art which demands variety, intelligence and the utmost patience. In 1973, Derbyshire, like others, were looking for an instant return in three-day and one-day cricket. In his three seasons with them, Venkat took 171 wickets, but they cost nearly 28 runs each, and that was a higher price than Derbyshire could afford.

He was not, perhaps, a wise investment for the county circuit, but Derbyshire appeared to have achieved the greatest of deals when they signed Lawrence Rowe for the 1974 season. Rowe was considered by many good judges to be the finest batsman in the world and there are many in the West Indies today who would still put him above Viv Richards. His Test debut was sensational, for he scored 214 and 100 not out for West Indies against New Zealand, in Kingston, Jamaica, in March 1972, and two years later he hit 302 against England in Barbados.

The cricket followers in England were excited by his arrival a few months later, but he never settled. He had problems with an ankle injury and with his eyesight. He failed to score a century, made just over a thousand runs and never played for Derbyshire again. Far from being the inspiration that had been looked for, he was a bitter disappointment, but then the whole story of his subsequent career has been that of a talent unfulfilled, even in his leading of the rebel West Indian side in South Africa.

With Rowe departed and Venkataraghavan leaving after the 1975 season, Derbyshire faced a dilemma. Their experiences with overseas players had not been successful, but now they produced a signing to match that of Rowe. In 1976, they engaged the South African all-rounder Eddie Barlow on a three-year contract.

Barlow had all the qualities Derbyshire most needed. He had been sought by several counties, but he had always declined to play county cricket. In Derbyshire, he saw a challenge. A medium-pace bowler and pugnacious batsman, he had played thirty Tests before South Africa's excommunication came, so he was rich in experience, but above all he was a fighter. He took over the captaincy of the county in his first season, and he transformed them. He spent hours working in the nets with players of promise like Miller and Hill, and he gave the side confidence.

His efforts brought no reward in his first season, but the county leapt up the table in 1977, when John Wright arrived, and played positive and purposeful cricket. Michael Carey was in no doubt as to who was responsible for Derbyshire's revival. 'The key to it all was Barlow's charismatic captaincy. Derbyshire did not lean heavily on his skill as a player, for though he emerged as the county's leading catcher and frequently chipped in with valuable wickets, he was often painfully out of form with the bat. Yet he welded what had been a collection of individuals into a team, starting with a winter fitness programme which produced not only stamina but discipline and self-confidence and, therefore, greater quality and consistency throughout the team.'

In 1978, Barlow's last season, Derbyshire began the season in splendid form and carried all before them as they reached the final of the Benson and Hedges Cup, having never before got beyond the qualifying rounds. At Lord's, their form deserted them, and Kent won easily, but Barlow had taken a side from the dregs and taught them to believe in themselves. The county implored him to remain, but three years was the time he had allotted, and he was, in any case, 38 years old. He had shown Derbyshire how to become a fit and positive cricket team, and when, three years later, with Wright and the immaculate South African batsman Peter Kirsten to the fore, they won a memorable NatWest Trophy Final on the last ball of the match, it was part of his legacy.

It is apparent that a pattern has emerged in the overseas cricketers who have been imported into English cricket. It is the South African born players who have made the strongest impact on the county game. The reasons are obvious. Deprived of an opportunity to play Test cricket, they committed themselves fully to the only arena in which they could show the world their talents. They were distracted neither by the adulation heaped upon the international superstar, nor by the endless round of enthusiasm-sapping Tests and one-day internationals. They had had no surfeit of cricket at the top level. They were eager for it. In 1970, South Africa was the foremost cricket playing nation in the world, the leading Test side, and its players have had to make do with the glow of that knowledge for the past seventeen years. In 1980, in the English first-class batting averages, four of the top eight places were taken by South African batsmen, none of whom, at the time, had played Test cricket. One of those four was Clive Rice.

In 1971 Clive Rice was named as one of South Africa's Five

Cricketers of the Year. He was a bowler of well above medium pace and a batsman of sound technique who worked hard at his game and was eager to play shots. He was, and still is, an all-rounder of the very highest quality. It was no surprise when he was selected for the South African side that was to tour Australia in 1971-72. The tour was cancelled and Clive Rice was never to play Test cricket.

He would not be human if, initially, he had not been embittered and frustrated. In an effort to develop his cricket in a world where he saw his opportunities diminishing, he accepted an offer to join Ramsbottom in the Lancashire League. In 1973, his club were beaten in the title race by just two points, and Rice won the highest praise from John Kay in *Wisden*: 'Ramsbottom kept on East Lancashire's heels throughout the season, because in Clive Rice from South Africa, they had one of the most successful recruits to the league. Rice contributed 531 runs and took 66 wickets to arouse the interest of several county clubs as well as the envy of most of his side's opponents. A talented cricketer and a likeable one, Rice did much to revive Ramsbottom's reputation for fighting cricket.'

Rice had no intention of playing county cricket, but at a charity match the following year, he was approached by Jack Bond, then managing Nottinghamshire, who asked him if he was the Rice who played in the Lancashire League. When he said that he was, Bond offered him an engagement with Notts in succession to Gary Sobers. He found the challenge of following Sobers irresistible. Few cricketers have been paid a greater compliment.

We have noted previously that Notts had failed to respond to the presence of Sobers in the latter part of his time with them, finishing bottom of the county championship in 1973 and third from bottom in 1974. Rice's arrival brought an instant improvement, and when that steady improvement came to a halt in 1977 with Notts finishing bottom in the championship, no blame could be attached to Rice, for he won the Wetherall Award as all-rounder of the year. He was the county's leading batsman and bowler in all types of cricket. Without him, Notts cricket would have been a shambles, and the county realised this, appointing him captain for 1978.

Before he could take up his appointment, however, he became involved with World Series Cricket, and Notts announced that he was to be replaced and that they had signed Richard Hadlee, the New Zealand all-rounder. The legal matters related to the Packer affair were cleared up, and Notts found themselves, rather fortuitously, with two of the best all-rounders in the world in the same side. Hadlee's appearances in 1978 were limited because of his involvement with the New Zealand tourists. Rice was top of the national batting averages. Notts rose to seventh in the table, and Rice was named as cricketer of the year.

He was reinstated as captain in 1979 mid-way through the season, and in 1980 Notts finished third in the championship, the highest position that they had occupied for 51 years. It was Rice's leadership as well as his own personal contribution with bat and ball, though hampered by injury, that brought about the change. He is a man who is strict in his application to the game, determined, intelligent and resourceful. A polite and gentle man, he despairs at the lack of endeavour and the air of complacency of many of the English players he sees around him.

When Ian Gould was free to leave Middlesex, Notts made enquiries about him. Bruce French approached Rice and asked what would happen to him if Gould came. 'I told him the matter was in his own hands,' says Rice. 'The next match he was magnificent, and he has not put a foot wrong since. You could leave him out for nobody, but any young player's future is in his own hands. He must practise and apply himself.'

Hadlee has an equally serious attitude to the game, and the two became firm friends. If there is a weakness in the Notts system, it is that too much has been left to them, and that there are other players, particularly bowlers, who could have given more, but have tended to hide behind Rice and Hadlee.

With Rice and Hadlee in harness, Notts recaptured the great days of Larwood and Voce. In 1981, Rice and Hadlee took Notts to their first championship for 52 years. *Wisden* lauded special praise on Rice, 'the most complete player in world cricket'. The following season, they reached the final of the Benson and Hedges Cup. In 1984, they lost the championship on the last ball of the season, and in 1985, they were back at Lord's for the NatWest final.

In 1984 Richard Hadlee became the first player for seventeen years to complete the 'double' when he hit 1,179 runs and took 117 wickets, and Notts failed by the narrowest of margins to win the county championship. Needing 297 to beat Somerset on the last afternoon of the season, Notts, with Rice hitting 98 off 109 balls, lost by 3 runs. The previous season, when Hadlee was with the New Zealand tourists and Rice was absent for much of the time after an operation on his hand, Notts had finished fourteenth.

One can hardly imagine what Nottinghamshire cricket would have been like in the past decade without these two fine players. The club has done its utmost to encourage young talent, and Rice will give a first team place to anyone who is good enough and works hard enough. To Broad, Robinson and Newell, he has been an immense help, for they have worked hard at their game.

There is no better captain in world cricket than Clive Rice, no more demanding task-master. He and Hadlee have set standards at Notts which, if they were followed and emulated, would raise the level of the game in professional accomplishment. It is not simply natural ability that has lifted Hadlee to his position of eminence, but hard work. Few fast bowlers have been so ready to pound the streets at six in the morning or torture themselves in the gymnasium for a couple of hours a day throughout the winter. At the end of the 1986 season, it was doubtful whether Rice and Hadlee would return to Notts for another season, and the county was doing all it could to persuade them to come back. In contrast, Somerset had announced that Richards and Garner would not be re-engaged, a statement that caused a debate of the greatest intensity in the cricket world.

It is worth examining some of the details that led up to this momentous decision.

Viv Richards was born on 7 March 1952. He made his debut for Leeward Islands against Windward Islands when he was nine-teen, and he was invited to qualify for Somerset in 1973. Somerset already had Hallam Moseley, who had some difficulty originally in obtaining an entry permit to Britain, as an overseas player, so they were told that Richards would complete their allocation. They were also told that Richards could not return to play for Leeward Islands in the winter of 1973-74, the period of his qualification, unless he received an official invitation from the West Indian Board. He did receive an invitation and was picked for the Combined Leeward and Windward Island side for the Shell Shield competition. He topped the batting averages with 270 runs, average 38.57. When he made his debut for Somerset in 1974 he had played just nineteen first-class matches, scored 920 runs, average 27.87, and he had not hit a century.

In his first year with Somerset, he played in 23 first-class games, topped a thousand runs, hit 107 against Yorkshire and 102 against Gloucestershire, played in all the one-day competitions and made a great impact. He glowed with good humour and had a constant desire to hit the ball hard which won him the highest admiration. He was taken to heart, and he was a favourite from the start.

On the strength of his showing with Somerset and his promise in the Shell Shield, he was taken on the West Indies tour of India and Pakistan. He and Roberts were the first Antiguans to be chosen for a West Indian party. The intention was not to play Richards in the Test side, but to allow him to gain valuable experience. It did not work out in that way. Injuries and form allowed him a place in the first Test in India. He failed, but in the second Test he hit 192 not out and one of the most spectacular careers in Test match history was launched.

Exciting as Richards's progress was, he did not begin to dominate the county scene until 1977. He performed magnificently for the West Indies in England the year before this, and from that time, given the uniqueness of his style, was the complete player. He was now joined in the Somerset side by Joel Garner, a giant and awesome fast bowler, and the county began to threaten for honours.

In fact, Somerset had finished second in the John Player League in Richards's first season, 1974, and were runners-up again in 1976 when he was with the West Indian team. They were runners-up in the John Player League for the third time in 1978, when they were also beaten finalists in the Gillette Cup.

Somerset won the first honours in their history in 1979 when they took the Gillette Cup and the John Player League on successive days in September. In the quarter-final of the Gillette Cup, against Kent at Taunton, the home side looked well beaten, but Joel Garner turned in a bowling performance of frightening pace and accuracy, took five for 11, and won the match against the odds. He was again to the fore in the final, when he wrecked the Northants lower order and took six for 29, although the man-of-the-match award went to Viv Richards for his breathtaking 117.

Both men were with the West Indian team in 1980, but Somerset moved up the championship table to fourth and were runners-up again in the John Player League. The following season the county won the Benson and Hedges Cup for the first time, and Richards clouted a record 132 in the final. Again they were second in the Sunday league. They retained the Benson and Hedges Cup in 1982 in a disappointing final against Notts.

The inevitable second place in the John Player League came again in 1982, but the county began to slip down the championship table, and some of the sparkle had gone.

With Garner and Richards on duty with the West Indies, Martin Crowe, the young New Zealander, was engaged for the 1984 season. He hit 1,870 first-class runs and took 44 wickets, as well as performing well in the one-day matches. In 1985, with both West Indians back and Richards scoring freely, including an innings of 322 against Warwickshire at Taunton, Somerset challenged for nothing and finished bottom of the county championship. There was a crisis in the county. Botham resigned as captain and was replaced by Peter Roebuck.

By this time, Richards had played in 77 Test matches, but since qualifying for Somerset he had played only seventeen matches in the Shell Shield competition in the Caribbean over a period of eleven seasons. He played more than that in his first season for Somerset. It is obvious that the competitive practice that he had needed to bring his game to its very high level had been provided by Somerset and the game in England. He had done much for Somerset, but Somerset had done much for him.

Since reaching his peak as a batsman, Richards had been on almost constant duty at international level, and the county game began to drag on him as it had done on Barry Richards some years earlier. There were days when the great Viv sparkled, but there were others when he lost sight of the needs of his side.

In July 1985 he and Garner were due to play for Somerset against Essex at Southend. Neither reached Southend, saying that they were unfit, although, reputedly, they had left Taunton fit to play. Vic Marks, captain of Somerset in that match, when asked if the West Indians would be playing at Lord's on the Saturday, replied that he wasn't too sure who had been playing *that* day. One Essex player commented, 'Thank God, we've never had any stars.' Nigel Popplewell made the highest score of his career in the match at Southend and a few days later announced he was leaving first-class cricket. He was later to speak on behalf of the committee's decision not to re-engage the West Indian pair, and he talked of the dreadful atmosphere in the dressing-room.

In contrast, a year later, when Richards did not play against Middlesex at Lord's, a spectator asked to have his money refunded, and his request was granted.

When Essex approached Martin Crowe in 1986, after Allan Border had stated that he would not be returning, Somerset were placed in a position where they had to act immediately. Incidents like the one at Southend in 1985 had soured relationships within the team. The top players seemed to be a club on their own, and the youngsters were being allowed to wallow. The county was littered with young players of promise who had not made the grade because they had received neither the advice nor the encouragement from the direction to which they looked for it most. Cricket relies on brilliant individual performances, but it is still essentially a team game. The problem that confronted Somerset was whether the star should be the servant or the master. Essex, for whom success had continued unabated, had answered that question long since.

Martin Crowe was contracted to Somerset until the end of 1986, and the county wished to retain his services. Under the regulations, they could play Garner and Richards or Crowe. Garner, troubled by injury, was nearing the end of his career, and, if one is callous, he was expendable. It was a straight choice between Richards and Crowe.

None has ever tried to minimise the greatness of Richards as a player, but set against this was the feeling that the glowing humour of 1974 had become a contemptuous arrogance in 1986.

Perhaps it is inevitable when a player has been so superior to his contemporaries. Crowe, on the other hand, had emerged as a batsman of the highest quality, dedicated and committed. As a New Zealander, touched by the first flush of success at international level, he was hardly likely to become satiated by the triumphs that have attended the West Indians over the past decade.

Moreover, Crowe's record at Somerset as a club man was exemplary. In 1984, on his own initiative, he organised the young players who he thought were drifting aimlessly and lacking self-respect. He established a dining brotherhood of the uncapped players and set them a motto – 'Strive for perfection in search of a cap'.

From the committee's point of view, there were other things that were best left unsaid and have remained unsaid, but it is strange, at a time when so many complaints are levelled against overseas cricketers and the detrimental effect that they have on English cricket by being allowed to play in county sides, that the biggest rumpus in the game for years should come because two of them were not being re-engaged.

The debate cannot be resolved to the satisfaction of all. Yorkshire have remained firm that only Yorkshiremen shall play for the county, but the world still awaits the first Yorkshireman of Indian or West Indian parentage to appear for the White Rose. Members of the Yorkshire committee will say that they have tried to encourage this new generation, but none has yet come forward.

It is an inescapable fact that every overseas cricketer who plays in the county championship means one less English-born player, and this is likely to hinder the development of some young players, but this must be balanced against the advantages. Cricket is more entertaining, more avidly followed and, arguably, a better game than it was before 1968, at least in the years immediately preceding 1968. We boast of it, too, as a humanising game, and in a world where we are striving to break down social barriers and move towards a universal society, it has a part to play in bringing people closer together.

In the 1930s, those cricketers whose names conjured up visions of greatness – Bradman, O'Reilly, Headley, Constantine – all remained distant figures, known from cigarette cards and newspapers, but, for most, ever out of reach. For the past twenty years it has not been like this, and the finest players in the world have been just a bus ride away. Had it not been for special registration, Procter, McEwan and Rice would have remained unknown to us, and our lives would have been the poorer.

For my part, I shall remain eternally grateful that I saw McEwan, Procter and Rice although I have never been to their country, and I believe that the excitement that Viv Richards and Richard Hadlee have brought to county cricket has enriched it. When Test matches and one-day internationals denude the county scene of so many fine players for three quarters of the season it is good that promising young batsmen and bowlers, denied the opportunity of facing Gooch, Gower or Botham, should be able to flex their muscles against Imran, Alderman or Clarke.

In the end, one must contemplate the reward, and decide whether it was worth the price.

Index